Wine Within Your Comfort Zone

Marla O'Brien

Earth Dance Press
Vancouver, Canada

ISBN 978-0-9939258-0-1

First edition

Library and Archives Canada Cataloguing in Publication
O'Brien, Marla, 1954-, author
    Wine within your comfort zone / Marla O'Brien.
Includes bibliographical references.
ISBN 978-0-9939258-0-1 (pbk.)
    1. Women--Alcohol use. 2. Drinking of alcoholic beverages.
3. Wine and wine making. I. Title.
HV5137.O27 2014   362.292   C2014-906614-7

Names and other identifying details of people interviewed or consulted for this book have been changed to protect their privacy.

This book is not meant to take the place of professional help for anyone who thinks they may have a drinking problem.

Cover and text design by Jim Bisakowski, www.bookdesign.ca
Editing by Joyce Gram, www.gramediting.com
Printed in Canada

Earth Dance Press
Vancouver, Canada
www.earthdancepress.com
www.facebook.com/earthdancepress
https://twitter.com/earthdancepress

In memory of my father and mother,
always and forever in my heart

To Barb,
May your glass always
be half-full !
Cheers
Marla

Acknowledgements

First and foremost I thank my dear husband, Tim, for believing in this project, and more importantly for believing in me.

To my three sons, Desmond, Jeffrey and Cory, your love, support and encouragement kept me motivated and strong. Without the influence of each of you, this book would never have been completed.

To the many courageous women whose stories unfold within these pages, you've reclaimed your inner power with dignity. Thank you for reaching out and making a difference to the readers of this book—and to me.

To Lisa Tener, the Bring Your Book to Life Program changed the course of my life forever. Thank you for your gentle guidance and support during the birth of the first completed draft.

To Joyce Gram, more than an editor, gifted in the art and mechanics of language, you have been an incredible editorial guide, even when our homes were 30 degrees and we were both melting. Thank you.

Contents

Women's Intimate Relationship With Wine

I have an intimate relationship with wine. I enjoy the warmth and silkiness of a gentle pinot noir streaming down my throat and entering my bloodstream. I revel at how it washes over my essence, bringing me to total calm. I let go of everything and welcome this euphoria. It is a blissful experience.

I used to enjoy the effects of wine so much that I would often have more than one glass in a sitting. Then I would continue to indulge, often subconsciously. I no longer do so. I've taken back control and reclaimed my will and my power. I am happier and healthier, and I sleep peacefully. Now when I enjoy wine, it's with intention and enjoyment. Now when I drink, it's within my comfort zone.

I am not powerless over alcohol, nor am I an alcoholic. I have no regrets about exposing my little secret to the world—that I've been a closet wine drinker for at least a decade.

In *Wine Within Your Comfort Zone*, I share how my intimate relationship with wine began to take over my life and what I did about it. I learned that drinking wine within your comfort zone means taking control over your drinking patterns and reclaiming your personal power. In this book, I share the tips, strategies and steps that led me to find my comfort zone and will lead you to yours.

Even as my wine consumption was increasing over a decade, two things I knew for certain: one, I would rescue myself from this oblivious relationship with wine; and two, I wasn't alone in this silent struggle. Many female friends, colleagues and relatives confided that they, too, enjoyed their glasses of wine on a regular basis. Yet they poked fun at themselves for having had a least one too many, too often. These women had created a daily wine routine that interfered with the quality of their lives. I have woven many of their stories, along with my own, into the chapters that follow.

The women I spoke with were hardworking, career-minded individuals, perhaps like you in many ways. I talked to women ranging in age from their late twenties to fifty-five plus: single women, single parents, moms at home, moms who work, grandmothers, mothers-in-law. It didn't surprise me to learn that more and more women are reaching for a glass of wine as a solution to the day's challenges. Many seek to fulfill a need, or to connect with other women, and over time find themselves on the dark side of wine.

As I created and implemented the strategies you will find in these pages, I discovered many wonderful truths along the way, and I'm excited to share them with you. While I do continue to enjoy a glass or two of wine quite regularly, I am mindful not to over-consume. This is my comfort zone.

CHAPTER ONE

Comfort Zone

Wine is bottled poetry.
Robert Louis Stevenson

Do you ever wonder, "Am I drinking too much wine?" If you do, then chances are you're drinking more than you should. Maybe you're beating yourself up about it too, and feeling guilty. Still, you don't want to quit. You simply want to control what you're doing and enjoy it—without concern or remorse.

Perhaps you find yourself justifying the glasses of wine you pour by telling yourself it's healthy. After all, medical journals say it's good for heart health, and Dr. Oz and his wife Lisa drink wine regularly, don't they?

You may have noticed how socially prevalent and acceptable it is to imbibe regularly, to pair your wine with delicious foods. And we're told how children in many European countries are raised on wine and live to be over a hundred!

Wine is made of grapes, grapes are a fruit and fruit is healthy, so you joke. Anyway, everyone's doing it. You're no different than your friends and the rest of society, nor do you want to be. It's social and it's harmless. It's not like you're belting back shots of vodka. Wine smoothes out the edges of a long stressful day and puts you in a relaxed state, quickly, quietly and without effort.

You may have heard that drinking in excess can increase your chances of developing certain cancers, particularly breast cancer. Even though you're aware of the dangers of over-consuming, you still don't want to quit. You simply want to take back your power and drink in moderation, without the guilt and shame, and more importantly, without putting your health at risk.

As I reveal my struggle, my story and my truth, you may catch a glimpse of yourself. The stigma society places on people like me had me believing I was powerless over my glasses of wine. This was not the case, as I explain. Through my personal journey, I have come to understand my intimate yet complicated relationship with wine, and I have relearned to drink in moderation. You can too.

The chapters that follow relate earthshaking, pivotal moments in my life. As you read them, you may be inclined to judge me using old dogma and a belief system saturated in outdated and irrelevant information. That's okay. No one can judge me more harshly than I have judged myself. All I ask is that you explore the truth—for yourself.

Chances are if you've read this far, your intuition is urging you to seek the truth, and along with it your power from within. As you will learn, your intuition, that inner guide you often hear and choose to ignore, will lead you to your comfort zone.

Wake-Up Call

There were several pivotal moments that shook my world and led me to take action and reclaim my power. Each of these wake-up calls had an intense effect on my inner spirit, each one significant and contemplative.

Awareness hit me head-on after an annual physical and the usual tests: pap, mammogram, blood, stool. Not expecting to hear back from the doctor's office, I was alarmed when the call came a few days later to set a follow-up appointment. I spent the next twenty-four hours in anticipation—and expected the worst.

The night before my scheduled appointment, a friend I hadn't seen in a while dropped by unexpectedly. "I've brought our favourite pinot noir," she sang, making her way to the kitchen. My husband had gone to a sporting event and would be home late. I felt grateful for the distraction of both my friend and the wine. The two of us picked up where we'd last left off, and the next thing I knew, we'd finished the bottle—and another from my wine rack. I barely recall her calling the cab. After she left, I stumbled into bed, set the alarm on my phone and instantly fell into a coma-like state. I didn't hear my husband crawl into bed. Nor did I hear him get up and leave for work the next morning.

Later, with gentle harp music playing from my phone, I woke abruptly and reached out to hit snooze, knocking the phone to the floor. As I sat up, the room spun around me and I felt remorse in the pit of my stomach. I started my usual routine of beating myself up for drinking too much and wondered how I would get myself to the doctor. I briefly considered postponing the appointment, but a shockwave jolted me to my senses.

I made my way to the shower, turned the water to extra hot and stood beneath the stream waiting for the dizzy sensations to wash down the drain. Once dressed and downing my second cup of espresso, I began to feel the caffeine run through my veins, bringing me partially to life. As I navigated cautiously to the doctor's office, just a ten-minute drive from my home, I contemplated sharing my secret with her—that I'd been a closet wine drinker for about a decade.

We Are Family

When I reached the point of wanting to reclaim my power over my drinking routine, I wondered how best to go about it. In search of a simple step-by-step approach, I was unprepared for what I was about to learn—that my intuition would guide me. I felt like Dorothy of Oz. I began my journey on the yellow brick road with hope in my heart that I'd find my way home. It wasn't until I had gone through some intense life lessons along the path that I found the truth—everything I needed was within me. All I had to do was tap into my inner wisdom. Where I once believed in old doctrines, as perhaps you do, this journey led me to trust my inner strength and, most importantly, to listen to my inner guide.

I have witnessed the negative impact of drinking alcohol in excess within my own family over decades of my life. At one time, my father fell victim to binge drinking while coming to terms with several life-altering circumstances. I share his story in chapter five to give credence to his ability to overcome life's challenges.

More recently, my brother passed away after a long history of drug and alcohol abuse. Sadly, he had somehow lost his sense of self-worth and turned to mind-altering substances to cope with even the smallest tasks. As a result, he saw himself as a powerless victim, and thus became one.

It doesn't stop there. Other, more distant family members have had their own confrontations with booze. Some of those who sought help joined Alcoholics Anonymous. However, for many, like my brother, repeated trials of this traditional approach to rehabilitation proved to be unsuccessful.

I'm guessing that you, too, can think of individuals close to you that have been impacted by alcohol in some way. Hearing the experiences and stories of countless others, I am certain everyone has been touched in some way by alcohol's dark side.

Considering my family history, it would be easy to credit old beliefs—to think of alcoholism as a hereditary disease. Have you ever wondered where this belief came from? While I don't intend to discuss alcoholism at length, or to define it, I mention it here only to clarify my own position. I made a decision to moderate my drinking. I chose to take control and to find my inner strength, while allowing myself to benefit from the positive aspects of wine. I believe that if I'd allowed myself to believe I was a powerless victim, not unlike my brother, I too would have become one.

What chance would I have to reclaim my power if I believed there was no hope, if I believed that alcoholism was a disease and hereditary and I was powerless? I chose to research the facts. I learned that this belief was deeply rooted in the early to mid 1900s, based on the times. What's more, it stemmed from the days of prohibition and thus did not come from any concrete, evidence-based research. This knowledge was the fuel I needed to begin my quest—to learn to enjoy wine within reasonable, healthy limits, in moderation and within my comfort zone.

Through pivotal events in my life, intuition screamed at me to dig deep and search for truth. I decided to peruse the self-help section of libraries and bookstores, reading everything I could find on the topic of women and wine. What I learned was not surprising.

Drinking wine is everywhere, every day, and in some way a lifestyle for many women and men. I have quite willingly spent time with friends, acquaintances and colleagues creating my own wine lifestyle. From planned vacations visiting wineries to sipping and savouring regularly, my wine experiences, over time, became a part of my everyday life.

Because I love cooking and everything social, I have a natural desire to play hostess and entertain. I have hosted countless events, from staff parties and backyard barbeques to girls' getaways and wine tastings. No doubt this was a contributing factor to my wine intake increasing over time. It also gave me an inside look at the relationship other women have with wine.

Many women who shared their stories with me also spoke of their love of wine and viewed their relationship with it as intimate. Many had at least some concern about the frequency and quantity of their drinking and, not unlike me, were in fear of others finding out. This brings us back to old belief systems, stigma and ignorance. I believe these factors have caused many women to go into hiding.

Fear of the alcohol label and society's judgment cause women to hide their wine routines. What's worse, women often begin to lie to themselves by thinking a daily wine ritual isn't a problem. Let me be clear: it is a problem if you keep trying to cut back and are repeatedly unsuccessful. Lying to yourself is where the real pain festers. It is in not telling, not sharing, your little secret— that you love your glass of wine a little too much, that you give in to it and give up trying to gain control. Please know that you always have a choice.

Society's general understanding about alcohol is that if you can't control it, you are an alcoholic and you need to get help from AA. I've learned through my personal experience that this is not the case, not for me and likely not for you.

When I began to observe, track and document my own wine routine, what I learned about myself came quickly. Not surprisingly, at the end of each day I'd find myself in the kitchen. I'd pour and cook, pour and eat. Then, following dinner, I'd pour and clean up. Yet all this pouring didn't appear to be affecting my job or day-to-day tasks. I didn't *think* it was having any impact on my family. However, I had this nagging feeling in my gut that these seemingly harmless glasses of wine could become a life-changing fiend.

Doctor Follow-Up

Once I reached my doctor's office, I let out a long sigh that gave me no relief from my hangover. As I waited in the tiny examining room, I observed everything in it. Beside me, a computer hummed quietly, its screen dark and hollow. A small hook by the door held a green hospital gown, and a mirror beside it nagged me to look within. I stood up and blinked at my reflection, feeling queasy and aged. I heard voices just outside the door and quickly sat back down.

The doctor breezed in. "Hi there. What can I do for you today?"

Confused, I heard myself say, "I'm not sure. I was called in for a follow-up appointment from my annual physical."

Sitting on her rollaway chair, she hit the space bar on the computer, bringing it to life, and attempted to distract my thoughts with small talk. Once she found what she was searching for, she let out a long sigh, sat back in her chair and said, "It's your stool sample. It came back positive. There was blood in it. You'll need to see a specialist, and I'm certain you'll need a colonoscopy."

If my hangover wasn't bad enough, this news made it even worse. My stomach tightened as I listened, without hearing, to the rest of what she said. She must have noticed my attention drifting. Clearing her throat, she brought me back into the room and continued to rattle off the possibilities, emphasizing one several times: cancer. It would be several months later that the procedure would reveal a couple of benign polyps, but no cancer. By then I had played out the worst in my head, so her news left me full of gratitude and well aware of how precious my health was to me.

Knowledge Is Power

Ideally, you have found this book before overindulgence in alcohol has caused destruction and devastation in your life. Wherever *Wine Within Your Comfort Zone* finds you, it is my sincere hope that it serves you well. I believe strongly that knowledge is power, particularly for women and their relationship with wine. The better informed you are about the negative impact of over-consuming, the greater your awareness and the more likely you are to drink in moderation, without shame, guilt or concern.

You may wonder:

- How do I deal with wine cravings?
- Will I need to change my social circle?
- Does it require a big change in lifestyle?
- How do I get my spouse on side?

For some women, learning to drink wine within their comfort zone may be a matter of tweaking weekend wine routines. For others, it may involve altering daily wine patterns. Any change will be unique to you, as you choose all or some of my suggestions.

You may also ask, "If I don't believe the quantity of wine I drink is a problem, why should I change my wine routine?" You may not need to change your wine routine, but the tips and strategies in the following pages may help you be proactive. You may also become an ideal role model for others close to you. If that's not enough to persuade you, consider this: you may not think you need to change your wine routine now, but are you willing to take the risk? Wouldn't you rather take action now to be certain your wine consumption doesn't become problematic?

The women who shared their stories with me also told me that drinking wine started as a casual affair, usually among friends, and seemed harmless. As the years passed, however, they stopped paying attention to the number of glasses they were pouring. Where once they had wanted a glass to sip, savour and enjoy, now they relied on it to transition from a stressful day into evening routines.

As you begin reclaiming your power, "stuff" will come up, obstacles and stumbling blocks. It may feel uncomfortable at times, but imagine this: you will not only reclaim your power, but you will feel a wonderful sense of pride and freedom as you do it.

Through the tips and strategies that follow, you will have the will and the power to decide when, where and with whom to delight in your wine. You will learn to savour it, celebrate with it and enjoy it to the fullest, as you drink moderately. And as you wear your new confidence, you can bet that people you know will notice. They may even say, "You look fantastic. What's your secret?" or "Did you lose weight?"

Step Outside Your Comfort Zone

Changing a routine or behaviour takes practice in order to master it and reach a goal. Old habits lurk and keep urging you to return. For example, if you decide to cut out your morning cup of coffee, you will no doubt have to fight the impulse to give in. However, if you practise an alternative, such as hot lemon water or a protein shake, and allow for some transition time, you will be more likely to succeed. Changing your wine drinking routine is much the same: you need to practise alternatives to support positive changes in your routine.

Through daily practice of new behaviours and routines, you will be training your mind and body to accept change. While you put your new routines into action, stepping outside your comfort zone, you will be presented with real opportunity to learn, grow and reclaim your power within.

Allow yourself the time you need to go through the Comfort Journal exercises presented in each chapter. Use these to guide your thoughts, feelings and emotions about your wine-drinking routine. Each of the exercises, tips and strategies will help to build your foundational support.

Acknowledge any resistance to change, and then let it go. If you slip up, get up, keep going and don't look back. Be kind and gentle to yourself and know that you *can do this*. Don't give up on yourself minutes before you reach a milestone.

When you feel you've reached a goal, celebrate by doing something special for yourself. Go to a day spa, shop for a unique jewelry piece, or go to a joyful place to reflect upon reconnecting to your inner power. Take time each day to acknowledge and show gratitude to your inner guide. Most importantly, give credit to yourself for every success along the way. Your comfort zone awaits you.

Keep a Comfort Journal

You may be rolling your eyes right now, thinking "I barely have time to pee, and you want me to sit down and write in a journal?" This book offers an empowering and comforting journaling experience. Here's how:

■ Journaling lets you explore, reconnect and respond to your thoughts. At the end of each chapter, you will find questions for reflection, designed to evoke your deepest thoughts and emotions. This warm-up serves as a lead-in to the journal-writing process. You may think it easier to simply sit back and think things through, without the writing follow-up. But if you do that, your insightful thoughts may get forgotten, without recourse.

- Journaling helps you release old beliefs that no longer serve you, guiding you to reunite with your truth. Following each warm-up activity, you will be gently prompted through the journal-writing process. The journal prompts are designed specifically to raise your self-awareness as you write and respond to the warm-up activities. When you are self-aware, you are better able to make decisions based on your core beliefs and what you know is best for you.

- I equate journaling with meditation, in that it has the power to transform mind, body and spirit. As you gain self-awareness, you become more mindful of your responses and reactions to your wine routine.

- Journaling teaches you about yourself in ways you wouldn't learn otherwise. Imagine journaling as a way of stepping outside yourself to observe, rethink and reevaluate what is important to you.

- If taking time to journal is a problem for you, then it's time to change. Some people write better first thing in the morning, others later in the day or evening. Choose what's best for you and make sure you are alert. You may also need to ferret out time gobblers like television, internet games or Facebook. If you commit yourself to journaling as though it were a natural part of your day, like brushing your teeth, soon it will be.

- Your journal could be a beautifully bound book of blank pages just waiting for you to compose, or a document on your computer. Perhaps you prefer a more decorative approach to help get your creativity flowing, such as coloured paper and pens to create mind maps or webs. One woman I know purchased a special box hand-painted with sunflowers. She used the box to store messages she'd written to herself, along with inspiring thoughts. Each message was dated and held a special meaning. Anytime she needed encouragement, she'd read one of her notes, reflect and then add a new one.

Comfort Journal Prompt

Warm-Up Activity

Consider the five W's for reflection:

1. **W**ho are you with as you usually pour? Your partner, friends, family? Or are you alone?

2. **W**hat are you usually doing while you imbibe? Cooking, working on the computer, watching television?

3. **W**hen do you most enjoy your wine? Do you have a daily or weekend wine routine, such as happy hour?

4. **W**here are you most often when you sip? Is there one place that stands out, such as at home or at a local bar?

5. **W**hy do you think you choose to drink? To relax? For social stimulation? Perhaps to boost your self-confidence?

Comfort Journal Entry

Once you have reflected upon the five W's, take note of any thoughts or emotions that arose. Use these to guide your writing. Did anything particular stand out?

For example, when I first reflected using the five W's, I discovered that I especially enjoyed my wine after work. Most often I'd drink at home alone while cooking dinner, my happy hour. This helped me relax at the end of a long workday. I also learned that weekends were very different. I was most often with my husband, family or friends enjoying a social evening.

———•◦•———

CHAPTER TWO

White Poison

Wine improves with age. The older I get, the better I like it.
Anonymous

Journal Entry, 2004

White poison is my wine of choice. I use it to relax, escape and melt into the end of each day. Each sip, each glass, each bottle is unforgiving. It has a mission of its own. It will try to consume everything about me. It will attempt to trick my mind first so that I believe I have no defence. It will make me think I'm power-less. When my guard is down, it will get to work on my body and the organs that give me life. Finally, it will strive to devour my soul, strip me of my will, my power and my purpose.

It doesn't know me, nor does it know my secret. It is fooled by my inner guide, crushed beneath the strength of my conviction and destroyed by the power within me. Nothing can invade my essence. As I live life from within and reclaim my soul, along with all else that is rightfully mine, I am free and unburdened. White poison will not own me.

This journal entry followed my fiftieth birthday celebration a decade ago. I wasn't hungover the next morning, and I knew why. I had slowly, over time, built up a high tolerance to wine. Although mindful of my increasing tolerance, I had a habit of silencing my gut when it told me to put the cork back in the bottle, even when I knew I should. This created an endless battle of self-sabotage and remorse. I had gotten to the point where I didn't know what was worse: drinking more wine than I should, or beating myself up afterward. My desire to consume wine on a daily basis was growing, and although it concerned me, I had not yet taken any action.

It's been said that fifty is the new forty, a turning point in and of itself. Fifty left me struggling with never-ending menopausal symptoms that included hot flashes and weight gain. Of course my wine intake contributed to these symptoms. It remained, however, an effortless way to cope with life's challenges. Both my parents had recently passed away, and my children were off to university and new jobs, leaving the nest and my heart empty. I began to question how I had gotten to this place of daily wine infusion.

From There to Here

As a young mom raising three energetic boys, I never thought about alcohol. My husband and I rarely drank, and the only alcohol we had in the house was a small bottle of Baileys given to us at Christmas. When we weren't with our children, we were catching up on much-needed sleep, leaving little time to do much else, let alone drink. Sure, we'd done our share of imbibing at parties and while attending university in our twenties. Once we were married with children, alcohol became incidental, enjoyed at special events like weddings and Christmas.

That was the early 1980s. We lived in a small northern town, family- and community-oriented, and were busy in a variety of ways. We enrolled our older two boys in everything from jack-rabbit ski lessons and skating in the winter to tennis and base-ball in the spring and summer. My intense involvement with the YM-YWCA as a community services coordinator and fitness instructor gave me a sense of purpose outside the home. My husband worked hard to support us while he climbed the corporate ladder.

On one occasion, Heather and her three children came for a sleepover. Both of our husbands were on overnight business trips, and we decided to have a girls' night that included all six of our children, ranging in age from two to ten. This was a new concept for us, particularly with children involved. The northern winter's chill had left us housebound, eager for adventure and girl time.

The technological toys of today didn't exist in the early eighties, leaving us moms to be creative kiddie planners. Prior to leaving on his business trip, my husband had been kind enough to rent a VCR and a couple of videos, doing his part to support our special night. The contraption weighed about fifteen pounds and came in a large, black suitcase. It took about twenty minutes to set up, if you knew what you were doing.

Heather and I managed to get all the wires plugged in and put on the first video while we cooked the kids' favourites—hot dogs and KD. It was important to keep them happy: happy kids translate into happy moms. No way did we want to surrender to guilt for rushing them off to bed so we could have some mommy time.

I had purchased one bottle of wine for the entire evening. It was white and crisp and would make this girls' night memorable. Once all six children were in dreamland, we cracked it open. As we sipped our first glass, we began opening up to one another.

A bottle of wine holds approximately four six-ounce glasses, allowing each of us two. At that time in my life, my tolerance for alcohol was zero, so when I was infused with the first glass and nursing the second, the room had already begun to spin. The next morning, I could not recall much of our intense conversation. Yet to this day, I still recall, somewhere through my second glass, gazing over at Heather and wondering how she had ended up with one eye.

At five the following morning, the youngest, Cory, emerged. I thought to myself, "Oh joy, of course it has to be my child to wake up at this hour." I brought him into my bed, rubbed his back and hummed a lullaby, but that only served to put me back in a trance.

Reflecting on all this, I can't help but smile. Even though two glasses of wine put us both under the table and left us with heavy heads the next day, I have no regrets. I'm clear how my tolerance has changed. Today, two glasses of wine would merely relax me and deliver me to a happy place.

As our children grew, needs changed, both ours and our kids'. The boys went from being spoon-fed to riding two-wheelers and having sleepovers with friends. Although a part of me yearned for "me" time, I was undeniably attached to my children. Watching them reach milestones was both uplifting and a little painful, as they took steps toward independence, allowing me to do the same.

Although I looked forward to the day when I would return to the work force, I feared it as well. I yearned for the adult world but was uncertain how I would cope with working, maintaining a household and parenting. Somehow, somewhere along the way, I'd lost my self-confidence. However, once all three boys were in school, I had the opportunity to reinvent myself. I eagerly bounded back to university to update my education. My self-confidence, ready to be reawakened, was keen to follow.

Not long after receiving my diploma in health and fitness studies, along with my teaching certification, we returned to the hustle and bustle of Greater Vancouver, where I worked part-time as a teacher. The boys settled into a new school with new friends and team sports, which kept my husband and me hopping in new ways.

Having lived up north for close to ten years, I hadn't realized how dependent my parents had become on one another. My dad had limited vision and was declared legally blind. He was the main caregiver of my mother, who was in the early stages of Alzheimer's disease.

I became torn between my new career and meeting the needs of my growing children and ailing parents. On occasion, these challenges clouded my judgment when I indulged in wine. The instant gratification of a glass of wine became increasingly inviting. Not only did wine melt away the stress of the day, it became a welcome, mindless activity, helping me put concerns and obligations aside, for a short while. I had embarked upon my journey to use wine to cope, and new events in my life were about to become a major influence on my increasing wine consumption.

Wining and Dining

As we moved along life's timeline, my husband became involved in his professional association. This required him to attend conferences and travel across the country. I had always been envious of his travelling, and finally the day came when I could join him. Not that I couldn't have joined him sooner; I just hadn't been ready to leave my children in the care of someone else.

Working part-time enabled me to book off to join my husband on many of these five-day trips. Conferences often included keynote speakers and educational sessions I was invited to attend. I became a sponge, taking in as much as I could on self-improvement and becoming Ms. Social Butterfly.

I welcomed the break from the routine of domestic duties, children's activities and my new teaching career. When my husband was at conference sessions, I took part in the activities for spouses, which included major attractions and sightseeing tours. Lunch was always a welcome treat, complete with wine, of course.

The conferences became a mini-vacation for me. I didn't have to cook or care about anything but my wardrobe, hair and nails. It wasn't long before I found myself relaxing into this way of life and enjoying the wine that was always present. Still, my enjoyment came from being in the moment, not from any strong desire—yet.

In the early 1990s, my husband was invited to North American industry events that, for me, were fantastic. The evenings involved delicious dinners with fascinating, wine-savvy people. It seemed that everyone's wine glass had a hole in it; the servers ensured that our glasses were always full. Never in my life had I been so catered to.

I still recall the first event I attended. I lost track of the number of glasses of wine I'd had. Still, I wasn't feeling intoxicated, probably because of the several meal-sized appetizers I ate while socializing. The dinner was impressive, but having had more than my share of appetizers, I could only pick at it. At one moment, I exhaled politely and laid my fork and knife across my plate. A lovely woman, wife of our host, smiled from across the table and said, "Wait until you see dessert." Fortunately, I wasn't a big dessert fan. But offer me more wine, or a double Baileys on the rocks, and I'm in. This was the first occasion I remember not wanting the evening, or the drinks, to end.

When I returned home from these events, I'd be exhausted from the continuous social interaction, not to mention the daily wine intake. All this was new to my body. I believe this is where I realized that I enjoyed everything about wine—the taste, the sociability, the instant relief and relaxation that washed over me. Wine was a simple yet glorious pleasure that soon became rooted within me. These years, although satisfying, took on a tumultuous side as I began to drink wine to take the rough edges off any stressful event that presented itself.

What started as pleasure at social gatherings, perhaps at the same time feeding my ego and needs, became years later a household staple. Not once during those years did I question whether I should be concerned about what this might be doing to me and my body. You may think I would have been more aware, being heavily involved in fitness and nutrition. But remember: I did not yet acknowledge that I was developing a regular wine routine. I simply enjoyed and welcomed the comfort wine gave me.

Wine Not?

These were my experimental and experiential years. In addition to the conferences and other events, I was introduced to winemaking through a friend. Winemaking became my new hobby, and I justified it by telling myself I was being budget-wise. In truth, had I been budget-wise, I wouldn't have had to justify anything, because the wine drinking wouldn't have been happening as often. I created the budget-wise winemaking idea at the same time as my intake began to increase.

My friend and I would get together to sip and sample varieties of wines, pretending to be knowledgeable oenophiles. With our mini-wine-glass sample in hand, we'd nod, sip, nod again, and comment: "A hint of cherry, wouldn't you say?" "Lovely, warm and buttery." As we played our connoisseur games, we'd make and bottle our cases of wine with the intention of creating collections for special events like Christmas.

We usually bottled our Christmas wine around the end of summer or in early fall so it would be ready on time. However, as the years passed, I found that many of the bottles I'd intended for Christmas were opened for Thanksgiving, then Remembrance Day, then any occasion I chose worthy. My intention changed— apparently. Now I intended to have wine whenever I wanted it, and I could create an occasion any day of the week.

When, as a responsible parent and daughter, I was attending my children's sporting events, looking after my parents' growing needs and teaching full-time, there had been no room for a regular wine routine. Once my children were driving themselves, however, I started opening the odd bottle during the week and having a glass while I cooked, as well as with dinner.

As my husband's career spiralled, so did his commitment to work. He was already commuting an hour each way, and now late afternoon meetings meant getting home even later.

Often alone, I began getting creative in the kitchen and discovered my love for food-and-wine pairings. I'd often pour a glass of wine while I prepped the food and another while my husband and I had dinner together. Still, as we continued to spend our weekends on the bleachers watching baseball during the day and basketball in the evening, drinking wine was more of a sporadic affair than a daily routine. In hindsight, I think this saved me from developing my wine routine sooner. Not attending a game was never a consideration. Had it been an option, and had I been powerless over alcohol, I would have stayed home and drunk wine.

When the day arrived that all three boys had left the nest, it wasn't long before I became the party planner, queen of everything having anything to do with women, wine and fun. The years passed and my wine consumption increased once again, along with my tolerance.

Wine Amnesia

One Sunday evening, my oldest son came for dinner. As the two of us sat comfortably in our tilted lounge chairs, feeling the warm sun stream through the maple leaves, I told him about a trip his father and I were planning.

"We're thinking of going to the south of France this May, perhaps Bordeaux. We would visit some wineries and small towns in the area. Your father wants to rent a car, but I'm nervous. You know how he is when driving in an unfamiliar place." As I rambled on, his brows narrowed into a concerned frown.

Finally, he held out his hand to me. I stopped, mid-sentence, and took his hand in mine, searching his gentle brown eyes for clues. "What is it? What's wrong?" I asked.

His response was slow and methodical. "Mom, you told me this last night. Don't you remember?"

I wished I could make something up, but there was no back-tracking from the truth. My lips twitched but no words came, and I struggled to regain my composure. No, I didn't remember telling him our plans. I didn't even remember being on the phone with him. "Mom, I'm worried," he said. "This isn't the first time. I haven't wanted to say anything up until now. I've noticed lately that when you drink too much wine, you forget things."

While I searched for some way to respond, hoping to put him at ease, he continued. "I'm worried you're developing Alzheimer's like Nanny, except that you're bringing it on yourself by drinking too much. I can't believe you'd put your own kids through this torment after knowing what that feels like."

I couldn't hold back the tears. He was right. I had caught myself on occasion trying to recall events of the night before. It didn't happen frequently, but it was enough to cause concern. What pained me more than anything was that my son had agon-ized over confronting me. His growing concern for my health and well-being was clearly evident in his distressed look. It was true: the more I drank, the more my memory was affected.

He hugged me, releasing an unbearable sigh of relief. This event was like a dagger through my heart. The shame, guilt and pain of his words led me down a dark, dark path to believing that my wine routine was out of control, with only one way out—AA.

Comfort Journal Prompt

Warm-Up Activity

Have you ever thought about how you developed your wine routine?

Find a quiet place to sit comfortably. Close your eyes. Try to recall the first time you tasted alcohol of any kind. Can you see yourself taking that first sip? What was your intention? How did it taste? What were you thinking at the time? How did you feel?

Now, try to recall your first wine experiences. How old were you? Where were you? Who were you with? What happened?

Comfort Journal Entry

Write about your early experiences with alcohol. Answer as many of the questions above as you can. How did you get from there to here, wherever "here" is for you?

———••—

CHAPTER THREE

Detox

One of the disadvantages of wine is that
it makes a man mistake words for thoughts.
                                        Samuel Johnson

Full of remorse after the confrontation with my son, I began to doubt myself. My daily drinking habit, while not *always* in excess, had led me to a dark place. I found myself sinking deeper into despair. Feeling as though I'd dodged a bullet with the cancer scare, I started to think my family history was catching up with me. Although reluctant, I finally shared my little secret with my doctor.

Through her referral, I ended up outside an office door with the word *Detox* written across it. I could feel my knees give way. I had completely given up on myself and believed this to be the only solution. I knew of no alternatives, and after all, this had come from my doctor. Surely she knew what was best. I would have to quit drinking completely and forever. I felt powerless, ashamed and addicted, and I had to go through this door to get the help I desperately needed. Or so I thought.

Getting hold of myself, I stepped inside the office. It reeked of cigarette smoke, even though there was no smoking permitted in the building. I approached reception and quietly announced my name and appointment time. Without making eye contact, the woman behind the reception desk checked off my name and pointed to a chair. As I waited, a toothless man with wiry grey hair, wearing jeans two sizes too big, talked away too loud on the opposite side of the room. Clearly, he wanted everyone to hear him. As he flailed his arms about, telling some story about his f%#king wife, another, older man sitting next to him, with glazed droopy eyes, listened attentively.

Just then, a younger, petite woman entered the waiting room. She, too, made it clear she'd arrived, bellowing hello and waving to reception. She seemed to know the man who was talking too loud, and sat down on the other side of him. This gave him a bigger audience, and he ramped up the volume. It was almost as if he was intoxicated, but I don't think he was. I wanted to disappear. It seemed like eternity before I heard my name called to go into the specialist's office.

The small room held many photos of African women and children, art and elephants, along with a World Unity symbol. They helped me relax a little. Nevertheless, the moment I heard the door handle turn, I wanted to make a run for it. The addiction specialist, a small balding man in his early forties, quietly closed the door behind him. "I'm Ian," he said, holding out his hand. "How are you today?"

Forcing a nervous smile, I lied. "I'm well, thank you." Then, in an effort to distract us both from the real reason I was there, I commented on the photos. It was clear he was proud to tell me they were part of a Christian mission to provide education and support in third-world countries. I listened attentively as he spoke about his travels and good deeds. Finally, he asked me, "How can I help you?" The tone in the room changed abruptly from friendly to serious, and my voice became paralyzed.

He sat down in a high-back leather chair, clipboard across his lap, and began to ask questions. How often did I drink? How much? Did I ever drink in the morning? Did I ever drink cough syrup or rubbing alcohol to get a buzz? Did my mother or father drink? Was I able to stop freely when I wanted to? The questioning seemed endless and without pause.

He flipped back to the first page of questions and put the clipboard aside. He didn't review them, explain them or discuss any impact they might have on a diagnosis. I thought, if alcohol is a disease, shouldn't we be discussing my diagnosis? And, if he has determined I am an alcoholic, shouldn't he be telling me my treatment options?

My thoughts were quickly squelched when he advised me to attend regular Alcoholics Anonymous meetings in the basement of the adjacent building. Almost systematically, he got up, walked over to a shelf of brochures and randomly selected a few. As he handed me the bundle, I had the gut feeling that it wouldn't have mattered how I answered his questions, his advice would have been the same.

I don't know what I'd been expecting, but I suddenly felt completely naked, vulnerable and broken. I had wanted so much for this man to give me a sense of hope rather than hopelessness. I was longing to discuss ways to cut back my wine intake. I didn't believe I fit the profile of an alcoholic, nor did he make any effort to discuss the term. Here I was, sitting in an addiction specialist's office being treated like an addict. My brother had been an addict. I knew what that looked like, and I knew how it could end. Most importantly, I knew I was not one of *those* people.

I'm not sure how I drove home through the tears and the sobbing, my shoulders shaking and my body convulsing. I told myself over and over again that I would never go back to that place. It had stripped me of my dignity, made me feel embarrassed, ashamed and worthless. There had to be another way.

Throughout this ordeal, a tiny voice kept telling me I did not belong there. That voice was my intuitive self. My inner guide was making an effort to lead me to reclaim my power. I began to reason: I've raised an active, busy family. I get up every day without fail, go to work, do my job and do it well. I've never missed a day of work because of alcohol, and I never drink during the day. The specialist's question about cough syrup came to mind. I thought, I don't even take cough syrup when I have a cough, never mind to get a buzz.

I had been writing in a journal on and off for several years. On the way home, I stopped at a stationery store and purchased a new, brightly coloured journal. In it I wrote these words:

> I am consumed by feelings of shame, embarrassment and guilt. By exposing that I have come so close to the dark side of wine, I'm more vulnerable than I've ever been in my life. I know I am not powerless over alcohol. I am not an alcoholic. Declaring myself a powerless soul would only make me feel like a victim, and I AM NOT A VICTIM! I am skilled, I am strong, I am powerful, I am determined, I am willing and I am ready. I can, I will, I must. I will trust my inner wisdom. I will heal myself. I can do this!

In sharing my secret about how much wine I drank, I lost faith in myself, just briefly. For a moment in the specialist's office, I lost my will and my power. Now, tapping into my inner wisdom, I believed I could get it back. Deep within, I knew that not always controlling my wine intake didn't mean I *couldn't* control it.

Seduced

Wine is a living thing. It is made, not only of grapes and yeasts, but of skill and patience. When drinking it remember that to the making of that wine has gone, not only the labor and care of years, but the experience of centuries.

Allan Sichel

The stigma society places, particularly on women, on not being able to control alcohol consumption is harsh, leaving many of us feeling ashamed, embarrassed and vulnerable. Yet, this same society strongly encourages drinking, promotes social acceptance of it and implies that it's the best way to have a good time.

Do you ever feel seduced by your daily, or periodic, infusion of wine? It is truly intoxicating, isn't it? Have you ever wondered why women have an emotional connection to wine, as benign and positive as that may seem?

Advertising giants, wineries, wine-pairing events and gastronomic displays—they all play a part in making wine look sexy. From the days of *Sex in the City* and Carrie Bradshaw came new cocktails, leading to today's concoctions cleverly named to attract women. Take for example the Juliet Romeo Cocktail, a James Beard 2013 cocktail nominee. Really? I had no idea there was such a thing. Some cocktails sound more like dessert, the Banana Cream Pie Cocktail for example, while others are pretty colours with girly names, pretending to offer status they can't deliver. Sex on the Beach? Can you guarantee that? Cocktails like The Dark Knight Rises Cocktail offer a knight in shining armour, while others like The Love Game Cocktail promise sex appeal. They come adorned with fruit kebobs and umbrellas to give women a sense of somewhere they'd rather be.

Similarly, winemakers have creatively marketed many of their wines to attract women. It's all in the name and the label: Mommy Juice, Girls' Night Out, Skinnygirl. Wines such as Fancy Pants flash vivid pink and turquoise labels, making them easy to find among the rows of wine bottles. I saw an ad for Skinnygirl, boasting 100 calories per five-ounce glass, yet it has no fewer calories than most wines.

Women meet for drinks just as often as for coffee. New moms create "whine" clubs and cocktail playdates with kids in tow, while the older, more "mature" woman is more likely to drink alone at home, wondering how her daily wine routine evolved. There are blogs about women and wine, such as Moms Who Need Wine and Pickled, and newspaper columns featuring connoisseurs flaunting their wine-tasting skills while popular chefs pair their choices with gourmet food—all while women sit and salivate.

The Grey Zone

After years of revelations that included family history, observations of women's drinking patterns, and countless interactions and discussions with women who enjoy their daily wine, I have learned the truth. Not everyone falls into one or the other of the two categories of take-it-or-leave-it or alcoholism. There is an area I call the grey zone. It's that place in between take-it-or-leave-it and alcoholism. In the grey zone, women receive warning signs, as I did, but often ignore them. Although intuition tightens in the pit of the stomach, they listen to ego, the pleasure centres, even when they don't wake up feeling well the next day.

We all know women who have the ability to take it or leave it when it comes to wine and spirits. They are often the designated driver who sips a virgin Caesar at a party. Yet these women also drink on occasion—a wedding, big birthday or other celebration. You know them.

Similarly, you can probably identify the chronic alcoholic. It may be someone you've seen on the street, dressed in tattered clothes, staggering their way through each day. Maybe it's a family member, friend or colleague who frequently drinks to intoxication with deliberate intention. These individuals are not grey-zone drinkers. Their urge to drink is powerful, all-consuming, physical and psychological. They are not likely to benefit from reading this book, because their alcohol dependency has become chronic, maybe even life-threatening. In no way do I advocate that an individual with a severe drinking disorder attempt to drink in moderation. In fact, it is beyond the scope of this book to address such drinking.

The grey zone is that place *in between* a take-it-or-leave-it attitude and being chronically alcohol-dependent. The women who fall into the grey zone enjoy their glasses of wine, regularly, usually at a specific time like happy hour. These women drink enough to relax but not necessarily to intoxicate. Women in the grey zone have a wine routine, an indulgence that needs some tweaking.

We all have our guilty pleasures. I love potato chips and could eat them every night if given the opportunity. In fact, there was a time when I did eat them every night, with dip, as I watched television. I ate them mindlessly as a form of comfort and satisfaction. I also enjoyed the salty crunch. It took some time, but I eventually broke my potato chip habit when I changed my diet in an effort to lose weight.

Women in the grey zone tend to give in to the evening at the end of each day through wine. They reach for a glass following a hectic day at work and drink while cooking and eating, sometimes when alone if they feel like it. Although able to designate themselves as a driver, abstaining on many occasions, they often choose not to. They'd rather take a cab or arrange a safe ride home. For many of these women, their wine glass has become an extension of their arm.

Grey-zone women enjoy the instant gratification of a daily dose of pleasure in a wine glass. Although it may have crossed their minds to cut back, grey-zone women usually repeat the pattern at the end of each day, finding it easier each time to slip into the routine of a wooden spoon in one hand and a half-empty glass in the other. Often, women in the grey zone try to fill a need deep within and are fooled into thinking that the wine will do the trick. Perhaps it does, but women know it's only a temporary fix, and the pattern repeats over and over again.

Tracking

In the 1980s and 1990s as a health, wellness and fitness instructor, I often mentored women on how best to get familiar with patterns of their daily indulgences. For weight loss, many agencies promote tracking food and caloric intake as a way to increase success. Jack Hollis, Ph.D., a researcher and lead author of a study published in the August issue of the *American Journal of Preventive Medicine*, claims, "Those who kept daily food records lost twice as much weight as those who kept no records. It seems that the simple act of writing down what you eat encourages people to consume fewer calories." Whether it's food, wine or a fitness routine, tracking raises awareness of daily patterns.

By taking a close look at all the habits and patterns surrounding your drinking, you can home in on what your next steps should be. These steps, taken a little at a time, can help you get back on track.

I used a tracking system to follow my daily wine routines and consumption. Tracking allowed me to look back on my day-to-day routine, as well as to see any patterns of behaviour out of the ordinary. For example, on days I worked later than usual, I consumed less wine. Tracking helped me pinpoint this pattern. Once equipped with this knowledge, I was able to rearrange my daily routines. That didn't mean I had to work late every day. Rather, it meant incorporating something new into my day, like a visit to my favourite bookstore, a place I could spend hours. In addition, keeping track of the quantity of wine I was drinking each day raised my awareness of each and every glass I poured, as I poured it.

There are a variety of methods you can use to track your wine patterns, routines and intake. It is important to use a system that is easy and realistic. It doesn't make sense to carry a notebook everywhere. Index cards are one option and can easily fit in a purse. However, while the cards are relatively small, they are also obvious, so not necessarily the best method if you are out in a crowd. Ideally, tracking should be discreet and convenient so you are more likely to do it.

There are applications you can download onto your device—Drinkcontrol, Alcodroid, DrinkTracker—which is ideal because not only is it discreet, but you're likely to have it with you at all times. Just google "alcohol tracker." Many of these apps will also give you an estimate of your blood-alcohol content, although I don't recommend relying on this and getting behind the wheel.

You could also text, email or voice-record your tracking information to yourself. If you have a smart phone, talk to your device. If you are out, you can easily use this system on your way to the washroom. Be sure to track each beverage prior to actually drinking it. That way you are not only being mindful of your drinking, you are more likely to be tracking accurately.

What to Track

- Day/Date: Each day is a new day. Be sure to record the date and day of the week. This will reveal any differences from day to day and on weekends.

- Time: Record the time you have each beverage. If you have your first drink at 6 p.m. and a second at 7:30 p.m., you'll be able to compare to another time when you had your first drink at 5 p.m. and a second at 5:30 p.m. and examine the circumstances.

- Beverage: For the purposes of this book, I am using wine as the example. However, you can easily adjust the chart for other beverages. I like to include the variety and brand name of wine I drink. In doing so, I have nailed a few red wines that simply do not agree with me. Don't lose focus on the point, however. Knowing the difference in alcohol content of wines is equally important. Some red wines are 12% alcohol content, while others are 14% or higher. The higher the percentage of alcohol, the fewer number of drinks you should have and the smaller your glass should be.

■ Quantity: Perhaps the most important aspect of tracking is how many drinks you consume over time. If you are having one five-ounce glass, be sure to record "1 – 5 oz glass of Pinot Noir," for example. If it's a 9-ounce glass, record "1 – 9 oz glass of Chardonnay." Be specific.

If you choose to use a tracking card, it can be folded on solid vertical lines in between each heading—day, time, wine, etc.—in order to make it smaller and more discreet.

For example:

Day/Date	Time	Type of wine	Quantity	Event
Mon. Mar. 1	6:30 p.m. 8:40 p.m.	Chardonnay Pinot Grigio	1 – 5 oz glass 1 – 5 oz glass	Home
Tues. Mar. 2				
Wed. Mar. 3				
Thurs. Mar. 4				
Fri. Mar. 5				
Sat. Mar. 6	6:00 p.m. 7:20 p.m. 8:30 p.m.	Champagne Sauvignon Blanc Pinot Noir	1 – 5 oz glass 1 – 5 oz glass 1 – 5 oz glass	Dinner Party
Sun. Mar. 7				

*Note: I would also include alcohol content and brand names, not shown on this chart.

Comfort Journal Prompt

Warm-Up Activity

Consider the following questions:

1. Do I want to reclaim my power and enjoy wine in moderation?

Consider what might be holding you back from getting started. Are your thoughts based on old beliefs and insecurities engrained from childhood, such as "What will others think of me?" or "Do I have the will power?"

2. Do I welcome change?

If you have difficulty with change, consider what your obstacles might be. For example, you may be wondering, "Will I enjoy myself as much? Will I make others uncomfortable?" Or "I don't have the energy to change. It's too time-consuming. I'm too busy to think about it."

3. Am I willing to change?

If you find yourself resisting change, think about where the resistance might be coming from. Look deep within and explore your feelings and emotions. What emerges about changing your wine routine? How important is it to you?

4. Am I ready to change?

Being ready to change means you are in a place of acknowledgement. You no longer accept things as they are. You are becoming more and more aware of the consequences of your actions. You know that if you wait for everything around you to change before taking action, you might never do it. You are ready for improved health, well-being and happiness.

Comfort Journal Entry

Make a list of what might get in the way of reclaiming your power and drinking in moderation. Opposite this list write how you might overcome each obstacle.

For example: Hectic day at work. Go for a walk in nature right after work.

———•••———

CHAPTER FOUR

Constant Craving

I cook with wine; sometimes I even add it to the food.
W. C. Fields

Making the decision to limit the quantity of wine I consumed ended up being the first step toward a glorious new beginning. I felt confident, motivated and capable. I also decided to implement an alcohol-free January to jump-start the New Year. In support of my endeavour, my family joined me, and this continues to be an annual tradition to this day. Alcohol-free January is not unlike eating clean to start the year off right. I call this taking a time-out from wine.

At the beginning of my time-out phase, I stood strong and shut out any inclination to even think about wine. Driven and motivated, I also didn't feel any major wine cravings at first. This surprised me.

As the month progressed, I did eventually come across some hurdles and annoying side effects. After years of this repetitive behaviour, I had sleepless nights, days when I felt extra hungry all the time, and occasional wine cravings that threatened my new-found determination.

Before this book was published, I asked a colleague, Ellen, to peruse a chapter. I trusted her expertise. Within a day, she called me and asked if she could share her story for the book. She thought it provided yet another example of women's complicated relationship with wine. This is Ellen's story:

> Working at an inner city school is not easy. Many of the children and their families live in poverty, and many of the parents abuse alcohol. My heart goes out to them.
>
> These children often do not make it to school until long after the bell has gone. Many get up on their own, dress themselves and get to school, hoping to have at least their need for breakfast met. My school offers breakfast to students in need, giving them a good reason to get up each morning. An older sibling will often escort a younger family member to school. It isn't unusual for some students to arrive at school in clothing that doesn't fit or is inappropriate for the weather, and often without socks, even in the dead of winter.
>
> I'd get home after each long day wondering if I'd made a difference. One Monday morning as I greeted my class, a six-year-old student took hold of my hand, looked earnestly into my eyes and said, "Ms. G, you're my special friend." The sincerity in his comment, coming from such a small child, warmed my heart instantly.
>
> I gave his hand a gentle squeeze and sensed a strong connection with this child. That evening, I tossed my coat aside and headed straight for the fridge. Without

even thinking about it, I poured myself an extra tall glass of my favourite chardonnay.

As I sipped, feeling the effects quickly take hold, I looked down into the glass and recalled the innocent look on the child's face. Like the parents of this child, my own parents had struggled to make ends meet. I remember many days getting to school hungry, dressed inappropriately, feeling embarrassed, unloved and neglected. I was left with emotional scars that to this day seem unbearable, yet these same emotions had led to my bond with this child.

In an effort to heal old wounds, as well as to honour the child's friendship, I decided to take time out from wine. Every time I had a craving after work, I would remind myself of the connection I'd made with him. Through imagery, I relived the moment he said, "Ms. G, you're my special friend." I found it comforting to recall the sincerity in his small voice and the warmth of his tiny hand. To this day, the image warms my heart more than any glass of wine could ever do.

Like Ellen, when I finally made up my mind to take time out from wine, I did crave it from time to time. Being mindful that the craving wasn't as much for the wine as for the routine and the relaxed state it put me in helped to keep me on track. After all, I had built this daily habit slowly over several years—it wasn't going to be a breeze to overcome. I found it interesting that I didn't crave wine all day long, and then, poof, a voice in my head spoke to me and commanded me to drink.

My wine craving usually presented itself around happy hour, the time I'd pour and sip the stress of the day away. Over time, my craving took on the form of an ugly little beast. Short and hairy, he was bossy, often convincing and occasionally able to charm me. At times he'd stand on my kitchen island, hairy arms crossed over his chest, bellowing, "Well, what are you waiting for? Crack it open!" At other times, he'd soften, appearing almost genie-like, and whisper, "Go ahead. One glass won't hurt you. Besides, after the day you've had, you deserve it."

Over the next few days, I noted a number of things about my cravings. The first craving came right on schedule at about five p.m. on evenings I was at home. If I was out, I was safe, but I knew I couldn't stay out all the time just to avoid the inevitable. I needed to tackle the little beast sooner rather than later, and stand firm. What became obvious to me was that I needed to change my happy-hour routine. Once I did that, I'd be squeezing the beast out of my day and he'd have no opportunity to lure me in. However, implementing change is not always smooth sailing. In an effort to hang on tight and control me, the beast changed his schedule.

I discovered, about two weeks into taking a time-out, that the first craving of the day hit me a little sooner than the usual five or six o'clock. The little beast had picked up his pace in an effort to throw me off and get me to cave. He was more stubborn than I. I realized that when I craved a glass of wine, I was really going through a physical and emotional reaction. While one part of me stood strong, the other begged me to give in. I began to despise happy hour.

When I found myself on the edge of giving in, I crossed my arms, shook my head and said, "Oh no you don't, you little beast. You're not the boss of me!" Making the beast ugly, hairy and short added a little humour to these moments and helped release the craving.

Cravings are annoying but fortunately short-lived. They have the power to bring on self-defeating thoughts and actions, if you allow them to. Cravings come at you in varying degrees of strength depending on your moment of need. This is where you have to make a choice—and take back the power. When you feel you need that glass of wine, it is your body reacting to the void, a little like hunger. Confronting the craving, feeling its effects on your mind and body, offers you the choice to release it. You can allow the cravings to control your actions so that you have that glass of wine, or you can let them go. When you deal with the cravings head on, you come to know them for what they really are, a physical response to your body not getting what it is used to.

I found that once outside the happy-hour time zone, everything got better. The anticipation and craving ended. I could read or watch TV without thinking about a glass of wine, and I felt stronger in a deeply rooted sense.

About three weeks into my time-out, I realized while loading the dishwasher after dinner one evening that I couldn't recall my last wine craving. Was it hours or days ago? I was sleeping better and had developed some healthier routines, like nature walks. I stood back and in my mind's eye watched the beast become smaller and smaller. Then, in the blink of an eye, he disappeared altogether. All this may seem like an oversimplification of the process, but I cannot stress enough how imagery helped me understand, confront and release wine cravings.

Time-Out, Stop Wining

Once you understand your drinking patterns from tracking, it's a great time to introduce a minimum of four weeks of total abstinence. Keep in mind that your body's response to abstaining from your wine routine is unique to you. Some women experience very little in the way of cravings; others have to work harder to release them. Withdrawing from wine is not unlike changing your diet. If you've ever been on a diet, you know how a craving feels and what triggers it. You may find your finger on the trigger, but you don't have to shoot yourself.

Go back and observe your tracking patterns. You may find that you drink wine more often at home or when you feel down, bored, overwhelmed or anxious. I was often anxious after work and found that a glass of wine helped me relax. As an empty nester, I had created a new routine that looked like this: get home from work, let the dog out, change, pour a glass of wine, start dinner. Cooking had become a mindless activity that included wine. Realizing this helped me change the wine routine into something more positive: get home, change, take the dog for a walk, start dinner. This one little change interrupted the pattern to the extent that it was far easier not to pour that glass—and the dog was happy too. I had delayed the process, decreasing my consumption.

As you track your wine routines, you may reveal possible triggers. Certain people or places may trigger a craving. Knowing what your triggers are can help you deal with them head on. I would talk with my sister-in-law on the phone one evening a week, getting caught up on our children's lives, husbands and work. I'd enjoy a couple of glasses of wine as we chatted. During my time-out, rather than avoid our conversations, which I looked forward to, I'd make tea while acknowledging the craving. Soon it was gone. Though uncomfortable at first, the more I focused on how my body was feeling in response to the triggers and cravings, the more I was able to detach myself from them.

Put your power to the test! You *can* do this. Don't try to confront all your triggers at once, as that could prove futile. Choose realistically and use strategies from the previous and following chapters to help you through those times when you would be inclined to have a glass of wine.

Being mindfully aware of your body and its response to change will put you in a position of power. When you feel the urge to pour a glass, stop and acknowledge the feeling. Breathe deeply and allow the sensation to pass through you. Resisting the craving will only make it worse—and invite the little beast to rear its ugly head.

Tips to Ward Off Cravings

A meal without wine is called breakfast.
Anonymous

To beat those cravings—and the ugly little beast—try some of these:

- Have breakfast for dinner. I'll assume you have wine with dinner and not breakfast, so make meals that do not go well with wine. When I have something like pancakes, waffles, or bacon and eggs for dinner, wine just doesn't taste the same and is easier to forgo.
- Eat dinner earlier. I used to wait for my husband to get home before eating dinner. As a commuter, he'd often not get home

until well after the normal dinner hour. I'd be home at least two hours before him, so I'd often be two glasses of wine into the evening before he even got home. I didn't like the thought of eating separately but knew it would be temporary and would help me. I found if I ate at five p.m. without the wine, I'd completely bypass happy hour. Once the hour was over, I was able to change my evening routine. When my husband got home, I'd sit, cup of tea in hand, while he ate and we shared our day. This allowed us to continue to have this time together.

- Don't have wine in the house, but if you do, leave yourself a post-it note. I have a post-it note on my wine counter and/ or bottle of wine listing three good reasons why I don't want to over-consume—health, memory, morning. I want to continue to be healthy, I want to remember the night before and I want to feel good in the morning.

- Be mindful of your feelings. Don't resist them. Acknowledge the craving for what it is, breathe deeply and let it pass through you. Inhale, exhale, release.

- Find a new hobby. I took up crocheting, something I hadn't done in many years. My hands were busy being creative, and everyone got scarves and toques at Christmas, even the dog.

- Get moving. Walking in nature renews your inner spirit—and will do more than ward off cravings. A daily walk in place of happy hour will help you coast through your period of abstinence. One woman I know started a walking club, which continues to this day. Whether you swim, cycle, walk or dance, doing something you enjoy will make for a smooth transition.

■ Visualization is a wonderful way to relax. It also has the power to distract you from thoughts about wine and relieve stress in your day. Refer to the visualization activity in chapter five.

Comfort Journal Prompt

Warm-Up Activity

How do you feel about going through the discomfort of wine cravings? What do you think about most? Think about a time when you wanted a glass of wine but couldn't have one. What did you do in that moment? What were you thinking? Explore your thoughts and emotions as you prepare to write in your journal.

Comfort Journal Entry

Set your date for four or more weeks of time-out and record it in your journal.

Write every day during this time. Include as many situations as possible, such as wine cravings, triggers, what worked, what didn't. Dig deep. Describe how you felt during cravings from day to day, then from week to week. How did you cope best? What did you notice?

———•◆•———

CHAPTER FIVE

Men in My Life

Wine has been a part of civilized life for some seven thousand years. It is the only beverage that feeds the body, soul and spirit of man and at the same time stimulates the mind...

Robert Mondavi

Although I wrote this book primarily for women, men also enjoy their daily glasses of wine. When it comes to drinking, men are often viewed as "hard alcohol drinkers." In their university party days, many engage in drinking games, usually involving beer followed by shots of hard alcohol, often leading to bingeing. As they mature and become established in careers, most men exit this phase.

I've watched my own three sons go from university party days to chasing dreams and establishing careers. Now, having a drink from time to time can mean sipping and savouring high-quality red wines, on occasion and in celebratory fashion.

It is often as couples that wine is savoured and enjoyed, particularly while socializing. In fact, wine is often the topic of conversation, with couples sharing and comparing wining and dining experiences. I've chatted with many couples who say things like,

"We're thinking of going to Tuscany. We're looking forward to wine tastings and pairing with delicious Italian food and touring the vineyards."

My husband and I are among these couples, as we will one day visit Napa Valley, Tuscany and Bordeaux. These areas, and many more, are conducive to the oenophile's affair with wine, socially, environmentally and culturally. Sipping and savouring varieties of wine is no different than sampling delicious foods specific to a region.

My husband is a moderate wine drinker, a take-it-or-leave-it guy and my biggest role model. He gently supported and guided me while I focused on controlling my wine intake and never played the role of wine police. His nonchalant attitude toward wine rubbed off on me. He'd make tea, invite me to go for a walk with him and the dog, and never hesitate to give me a never-ending supply of loving hugs. He has had a huge impact on my success at drinking wine in moderation and sticking to it.

Everything You Need Is Within You

My dad, however, had a different sort of impact. A gentle and kind man, he always put his family first. But Dad was not without his times of stress, and as a district manager for a large national company, these stresses began to test his inner strength as he reached mid-life.

I recall many happy times as a child. Dad would have the odd beer while watching a hockey game or working on his boat hoisted in the driveway. Yet, when he reached mid-life, something jolted him. A young teenager at the time, lacking much life experience, I didn't understand. My dad had learned that his oldest son was addicted to drugs and alcohol and deeply in debt.

This was the 1960s, when society scrutinized and judged others. A highly regarded employee, my dad struggled to deal with his emotions, feeling as though he'd failed his son in some way. Adding to his heartbreak, he was diagnosed with macular degeneration, a disease that would eventually leave him legally blind. He began binge-drinking to ease his pain, usually over a weekend so it wouldn't affect his job, but enough to cause concern and raise the question, Is he an alcoholic? Following is a letter I wrote to Dad as a young teenager during one of his binges:

Dear Dad,

You leave and don't come home, and then when you do, you are staggering and drunk. You slur your words and you look at me like you don't know who I am. I look back at you and I know I don't know who you've become.

I don't understand why you do it. I don't understand why you don't stop. Don't you love us anymore? Please, Dad, please stop drinking. You are hurting yourself and everyone who loves you. Mom and I love you. Do you know you are hurting us too?

I miss the times we would laugh together. I miss you taking Mom and me shopping on Friday nights. I miss you telling me to dress warm when I leave for school each morning and to sleep tight when I go to bed.

I'm afraid for you, but mostly I'm afraid for Mom and me and that we might have to live without you. I'm worried something bad is going to happen to you. Please, Dad, please stop. Please come back to us.

Always and forever your daughter, Mar

I placed the letter on his desk where he often worked in the evening and waited for his current binge to end. I didn't know how long he'd be consumed, this time. The usual binge lasted a couple of days, sometimes more. I waited for him to return to us, to sit at his desk, to be normal once again and sober.

That night at three in the morning, I heard him stumble to the bedroom he and my mother shared next to mine. I waited for the hum of angry words between them. Only silence followed. I breathed a long, heavy sigh of relief and let the tears flow freely onto my pillow.

The next morning I got up early, feeling numb and abandoned. I sat anxiously on the couch, waiting, my heart pounding through my chest. I hoped that when he got up he would notice the letter I'd propped up, in full view, on his desk.

He entered the living room, looking somewhat dishevelled, and shuffled to his desk. His premature grey hair, usually neat and slicked back, hung in strands on either side of his dark brows, and I could tell he'd been awake most of the night. Somehow, I sensed the dawn of awakening for him and for me. I knew he felt me in the room but was avoiding eye contact. He slunk silently into the chair at his desk, with his back to me, and as he did so his body stiffened and shifted nervously. He'd seen my letter. His right arm reached out to a familiar brass envelope opener. As he gently tore open my letter, I felt his shame.

I could hear my words flowing through him as he silently read my pain and recognized his own. He leaned forward, placing his left elbow on the desk and resting his forehead in his hand, and wept silently. A moment later, he tentatively pushed himself to his feet and turned, and our eyes met.

Without hesitating, I ran to hug and forgive him. His unshaven face looked centuries old, his green eyes swollen and hollow. In his shaky voice, he whispered to me, "I'm so sorry,

Mar. I have had trouble coping with everything. Please forgive me. You and your mother are my life. I love you both. There isn't anything I wouldn't do for you."

Although my dad did continue to drink from time to time, the bingeing ended. I often wondered how he shifted from being seduced by alcohol's potency to reclaiming his pride, dignity and power.

Looking back through the eyes of an adult, I now know he did have a lot to cope with. Not only did my brother's situation paralyze him, but he was forced into early retirement and placed on disability. This left him feeling disgraced and powerless over a diagnosis he couldn't control. Macular degeneration was slowly taking over his life.

In the early 1960s and 70s, there existed tremendous cultural instability in society. It was a time not unlike the series *Mad Men*, where smoking and drinking were accepted, even supported and encouraged. At every business meeting and conference, in restaurants and homes, many coped through excessive drinking. My dad was one of them.

What impact did his binges have on me? This question is not to imply fault. On the contrary, it is to recognize my dad's relentless determination to control his drinking. He dug deep to find the inner strength and courage to take back his personal power. In the process, he gained back the respect of his family—and became a hero in my eyes. He had used alcohol to cope through a very difficult time in his life, yet he managed to confront and defeat it.

My dad got up one morning and made a conscious decision to quit bingeing. As he healed himself, he never discussed his pain or symptoms of withdrawal, nor did he mention any yearning to drink excessively. He simply took control of his drinking, owned it and conquered it.

As my dad aged he drank less and less, and when he drank it meant one small glass of white wine or, on special occasions, a shot of whiskey. Once he was legally blind, he came to live with my husband and me and our three sons, while my mother went to a care facility because of the early onset of Alzheimer's disease. Despite all that had taken over my dad's life, he continued to enjoy an occasional drink, always staying within his comfort zone.

Alcohol once infused, seduced and intoxicated my father, but it never succeeded in owning him. Never did he seek help from external sources, nor did he see himself as a powerless man. From the time I was a small child, my dad taught me to look within for strength when I needed it. He'd say, "Everything you need to get through this is within you." He finally learned to listen to his own inner guide. Through his strength, determination and courage, I also learned to look within for my personal power.

Every Day Is a Gift

Not unlike most people, Shannon can recall a chain of relatives who had a drinking problem. She told me about the aunt with rose-coloured cheeks who always seemed giddy, the uncles from both sides of the family who enjoyed their evening tipple a little too much, and the cousins down the family tree who imbibed regularly. Not wanting to fall into the family mould, Shannon took her power back when she realized the impact too much wine was having on her mood at the end of each week. This is her story:

My relationship with wine began in university. A pleasant source of connection and relaxation among friends drinking wine evolved into a great way to take a break from writing papers and studying, not to mention exams. When I landed my first job in my designated profession, wine continued to ease my anxieties at the end of the week and often the end of each day. I noticed no shortage of colleagues who felt the same way.

One Sunday morning I woke up feeling completely overwhelmed. It had been a hectic workweek, but nothing specific stood out. It seemed that more and more often, the end of the week left me feeling gloomy. I had consumed way over my limit the night before and decided to go for a long walk to clear my head. As I approached the local park, I found myself hoping to find serenity. Surprisingly, I found much more.

The brisk spring air caught in my throat as I hurried toward a park bench that had caught my eye. I hadn't noticed from a distance but could now see that on it lay a cocoon of tattered blankets wrapped around what I assumed to be a homeless person. Peeking out from one end were his scruffy brows and stubbly beard. He lay there smiling up blissfully at the maple trees as though he could hear them revealing their secret. Too late for me to turn around, he found me in the corner of his crescent-shaped eyes. He wriggled free from his nest and sat up quickly, still wrapped in the warmth of his makeshift bed. I dreaded the encounter and prepared myself to ignore him. Yet something in his joyful face kept me coming. Without warning I heard him utter softly, "Hi there, lady. Don't worry. Every day you wake up is a good day. Every day is a gift. Bless you, child."

I didn't know whether to flee the scene or fall to my knees and thank him for his blessing. I couldn't believe a complete stranger had looked through my outer shell and realized my conflict. Completely overwhelmed by his comment, I couldn't breathe, let alone speak. Making eye contact, I kept walking, a little slower as I passed by him, leaving him with a grateful nod and a nervous smile.

Later that afternoon, I called a friend who lived in the same building. She suggested we go out to a local heated rooftop bar. We sat at a table by the edge of the deck overlooking the park. I couldn't see the bench or anyone homeless.

I ordered a glass of my favourite pinot grigio and spilled my heart out to my friend. I told her about the man in the park, how I'd been feeling stressed and unhappy.

With each glass of wine I consumed that afternoon, I emptied a little more of my soul into the conversation. It wasn't until much later, and two more glasses of wine, that I realized I was drunk. I felt absolutely spent and barely recall crawling into bed at 7:30 p.m. There is nothing worse than waking up on a Monday morning with a hangover.

Not able to shake loose the memory of the man in the park and his words, "Don't worry. Every day you wake up is a good day. Every day is a gift," I thought about the power of his message, and it played on my mind.

It wasn't long after that I decided to alter my approach and deal in a new way with how I felt at the end of each week. I had heard about visualization techniques and began using them to overcome feelings of melancholy. It has been a powerful and inspiring experience. I now feel connected to everything around me and often find myself visiting the library, rather than the bar. I choose inspirational books to read, and I enjoy green tea at my favourite teashop nearby. Although I continue to walk through the local park from time to time, I have never again encountered the homeless man. I can't help but ask myself what I would do if I did. Would I have the courage to sit down and talk with him for a while?

I now find my emotional connection to wine minimal, and actually very positive. I am far more aware of when and how much wine I drink on any given day. I have learned that I can connect and unwind in other ways, often among good friends, with or without a glass of wine.

Visualization and Vision Boards

The power of visualization can be incredibly uplifting. When I visualize, I often find myself near the ocean or sitting by a babbling brook, or occasionally deep in the woods. Any of the places I envision leave me feeling peaceful and calm. Getting in touch with my physical and mental wellbeing took time, however. Once I was practising visualization regularly, I found it to be my spiritual companion. Not only did I feel more grounded, I felt reconnected with parts of myself, both physical and emotional, that had not been in balance for years.

One compelling way to bring visualization to life is to create a vision board. A vision board is like a collage, with one big difference: You are not collecting pictures and phrases with any particular theme in mind. You are choosing them randomly and intuitively.

Here's how to create your vision board:

- Collect a few magazines you don't mind ripping the pages out of. As you flip through, try not to think of anything specific. Wait for something to attract your eye and pop out at you. When this happens, tear out the page or words from the magazine and put them aside. Collect as many as you can until you feel you have enough to fill your board. Boards vary in size. I suggest starting small, perhaps 11" x 16".

- Now you are going to groom and trim the pages and phrases you've put aside. Allow yourself to be guided as you place them on your board. What resonates with you? Are you grouping colours together, or perhaps similar pictures or patterns? Let yourself fall into the flow as you cut, paste and create. Glue the pictures to the board, and when you've completed it, keep it where you will see it on a daily basis. Use it to manifest that which you most want in your life.

- I have created several vision boards, each with a new inspiration. Many years ago I created a board with pictures of healthy food, women exercising, cups of tea and assorted books. I hadn't chosen the pictures deliberately, rather intuitively and randomly. I had no theme or expectation in mind as I collected words and photos. Once complete, I kept the board on my fridge for many months. Previous to this, I had been continuously discouraged by my ever-increasing weight gain. Within six months of creating my vision board, I'd lost thirty pounds. I cannot stress the power it held in guiding me.

Comfort Journal Prompt

Warm-Up Activity

Get into a comfortable position where you won't be interrupted. Softly close your eyes and focus on your breath. Keeping your lips gently together, breathe in deeply, opening the back of your throat and allowing the air to pass easily through. Exhale slowly, letting out any feelings, thoughts and emotions that no longer serve you. Once again breathe in deeply, opening your throat and allowing the air to pass easily. Continue to focus on your breath as you breathe normally. Notice any tension in your body. Focus on breathing through each tense area, one at a time, until you are completely relaxed.

When you feel completely relaxed, imagine yourself sitting in a quiet place in nature. This is your joyful place. Focus on this place, knowing there is only you and this moment in time. Listen carefully to all the sounds around you, both near and far from you. Hear each sound on its own. Do you hear birds? Waves? Leaves rustling in the breeze? Do you hear silence? Place your attention on how you feel. Are you warm? Cool? Hot? Do you feel a breeze? Now, what is the scent in the air? Is it the trees? The ocean? Is it the clean, refreshing scent of a meadow, or the deep, mossy aroma of the forest?

Imagine a sense of freedom. You are free to choose whatever, whenever and wherever you are in any moment in time. Feel the power within you. Notice how strong you feel. Be mindful of your body and thank it for the job it does keeping you strong and healthy. Thank your inner guide for the intuition that guides you, for the wisdom that confirms what you already know, and for the strength that lets you persevere.

Place your focus back on your breath. When you are ready, slowly open your eyes and gently breathe in and out until you feel ready to move. Then begin slowly with your toes and move up your body. Take a moment to rest and return to the present moment.

Comfort Journal Entry

Now write about your joyful place and how it made you feel. Write down anything from your five senses and beyond that you noticed. Can you visualize your life after you've accomplished your goal to cut back on the wine you drink? Where did your visualization take you? What did you feel, hear, see, smell, taste?

CHAPTER SIX

Know Your Limit, Wine Within It

There are two reasons for drinking wine . . .
when you are thirsty, to cure it; the other, when you are not thirsty,
to prevent it . . . prevention is better than cure.
Thomas Love Peacock

At this point, you have recorded entries in your journal, tracked your drinking patterns and taken note of what specifically triggers you to even think about wine. In chapter four I suggested taking time out from wine for four or more weeks. As you progress through the time-out phase, you will have a real sense of what your wine cravings feel like and how you handle them best. Congratulations! You are on your way to a new and improved relationship with wine!

Every time I discuss the importance of enjoying wine within personal limits, a friend's daughter, Mary, comes to mind. Mary had an eye-opening experience as she enjoyed a girls' night with friends she hadn't seen since moving to the country. The following incident left Mary with an unwavering conviction that when she drank wine, she would always stay within her limit, no exceptions.

Emergency Room

Mary and her husband lived in the countryside outside the city limits. They both commuted to work, but occasionally Mary's husband would be called out of town on business and she'd be left alone.

During those times, Mary felt lonely. She missed her friends and the drinks they had shared before she and her husband bought their first home. Yearning for a girls' night, Mary decided to invite her friends over while her husband was away.

With excited anticipation, the five women juggled appetizers, overnight bags and copious quantities of wine as they zigzagged up the driveway. The evening, well underway with grown-up girls giggling, sipping wine and grazing on appetizers, filled Mary's loneliness. Happily, Mary busied herself heating up snacks while sipping a glass of chardonnay mixed with soda water and ice, often called a wine spritzer.

Months earlier, Mary had decided to limit her wine to two drinks on any occasion, with no exceptions. She began cutting back, hoping to become pregnant in the near future. And she knew she wouldn't drink at all during the pregnancy.

When one of the girls offered to top up Mary's wine glass, she quickly placed her hand over the top. "No thanks. I need to pre-pare myself for motherhood." Practically falling off the kitchen bar stools, the young women squealed with delight, hugging Mary a little extra tight at this news.

Mary appreciated the support of her friends and encouraged them to enjoy their wine and have fun. Although she wanted to enjoy wine with her friends, it held little importance to her com-pared to the desire to conceive. Plus, while thoroughly enjoying the company of her guests on a new level, Mary knew she'd wake up the next day feeling great.

Later that evening, when getting ready for bed, one of the women, Linda, said she didn't feel well. Within minutes the others could hear her throwing up in the bathroom. They empathized but passed it off as too much wine. "Linda doesn't usually drink that much, poor thing," one of the girls remarked.

When Linda came out of the bathroom, she keeled over, holding onto her abdomen, moaning and in obvious pain. Mary sensed the seriousness of the moment. Calling an ambulance would have meant waiting longer to get her to the hospital than if Mary drove. In that moment, Mary felt relieved that she had had only one glass and it had been diluted.

The other women remained at the house while Mary drove to the hospital. The emergency room nurses admitted Linda immediately, and it wasn't long before the doctor performed an emergency appendectomy.

After the surgery, Mary learned that Linda would have been much worse off had she not gotten to the hospital when she did. For Mary, this experience reconfirmed the importance of drinking within her limit.

Understanding Your Limits

Before you run out the door to buy a bottle of your favourite chardonnay to celebrate your period of abstinence, consider getting to know the reasons for limiting yourself in the first place. Also consider allowing a wine situation to present itself to you, rather than the other way around.

A little research can go a long way in helping you understand the health aspects of limiting your wine intake. Learning about blood alcohol levels and their effects on mind, body and spirit helped me determine boundaries and stick to them.

According to North American standards, one five-ounce glass of wine per day is considered a healthy dose. It stands to reason that the less you weigh, the less you should consume. Also, for the average woman it takes at least an hour for that five-ounce glass of wine to be processed by vital organs in your body. Best to let it do so before pouring yourself another. If you have two glasses within an hour, you're definitely going to increase your blood alcohol level more quickly than if you spread those two glasses over two or three hours. You will also feel the effects more quickly if you consume too much too fast. If you don't feel the effects, it may be because you have increased your alcohol tolerance through over-consuming on a regular basis. According to research, it doesn't take much to get there.

In their book *Controlling Your Drinking: Tools to Make Moderation Work for You*, authors William R. Miller, Ph.D., and Ricardo F. Muñoz, Ph.D., claim, "Tolerance (being able to 'hold your liquor') is usually not a good thing. You need ever larger doses of alcohol to experience the same effect, but your body still has to process it all."

People with a high tolerance for alcohol have acquired this tolerance through over-consuming. The authors also suggest that those of us with a high tolerance tend to drink too fast and need to slow down: "Even having one drink decreases your response to the next drink. It's that fast. When you drink more, your tolerance increases. As you cut back on drinking, your tolerance decreases."

Through their research and scientific data, Miller and Muñoz clearly differentiate between men and women and body weight and age, offering physiological explanations and several case studies to back up all their findings.

On treatment alternatives for alcohol overuse, Gabrielle Glaser doesn't hold back in her book *Her Best Kept Secret*. She backs up all her investigative efforts with research, women's accounts and comparative analysis, using her expertise as a journalist to make some powerful points.

Glaser talks about the health profession's one-size-fits-all remedy for alcohol abuse, not unlike the AA prescription I was once given. She says there is no scientific basis for the term *alcoholic*, nor are there what may be considered best practices in treatment alternatives. Furthermore, no one seems to agree on what a healthy daily dose of alcohol should be: "From Sweden to Australia, Denmark to South Africa, drinking recommendations for women are twice the amount health officials suggest for American women." Consumption for women also varies from country to country: "In Spain . . . the recommendation for women is to consume no more than . . . three five-ounce glasses of wine a day . . . a glass of wine at lunch, as aperitif with a snack and a glass of wine at dinner." When you combine this information with the research in *Controlling Your Drinking*, which says that it takes at least an hour for your body to process one drink, it starts to make sense to drink wine differently.

Glaser makes a strong point about the lack of scientific evidence regarding women, alcohol consumption and drinking in moderation. *Her Best Kept Secret* is an eye-opener on women, wine and alternatives to cutting back or quitting altogether.

Equally important is the question of drinking in moderation in relation to addiction models. In their book *Recover*, Stanton Peele, Ph.D., and Ilse Thompson write about how popular addiction mythology emphasizes the drug or behaviour itself and insists that addicts admit to being powerless over the thing they are addicted to. These authors say that the claim that abstinence is the only option to recovery is backwards. Considering that I am living proof that it is possible to recover from the habitual or addictive aspect of wine, I wholeheartedly agree with Peele and Thompson when they say, "If you are no longer addicted, and you have healthy coping strategies, there is no drug that can render you helpless before it."

On drinking in moderation, Peele and Thompson go on to say, "Moderation is indeed possible for people who have truly recovered from addiction. You may be able to look forward to drinking a glass of wine . . . with your friends without fear of ruining your life."

Peele and Thompson say it's quite possible to imbibe from time to time while tapping into your inner wisdom: "Aiming for moderation requires self-knowledge. Someone who drinks addictively sometimes, but who also has the capacity to enjoy wine with dinner or with friends, has a good reason to see moderation as a recovery goal. It contributes value to his [or her] life."

For me, drinking in moderation means a limit of two glasses of wine per day and nine per week. This is not to imply that I actually have two a day. Rather, this is my maximum on any day and any occasion, with no exceptions. I have found it important to have days without wine and to make this a ritual rather than allow any new or old wine routines to emerge. This has served me well, preventing me from exceeding my limit or going back to the habitual behaviour I once engaged in.

If you do your own research, you are likely to discover what I did: there is a discrepancy in what is considered drinking in moderation and daily allowances. You may think a limit of two glasses a day allows you to drink fourteen per week. Not true. You can drink two glasses in a day, just not every day. If your limit is one five-ounce glass per day, with no more than seven per week, consider Saturday no different than Monday. Also, you need to incorporate days without wine, where you are engaged in other healthy activities.

When your month of abstinence is over, welcome the moment when you have a glass of wine. Allow it to come to you, rather than deliberately creating an excuse to drink. Resist over-emphasizing your first glass of wine after a few weeks off. While it's human nature to want something to look forward to, do your best to keep it casual. Stroll into the moment wearing a take-it-or-leave-it attitude. Sit down, order or pour your five-ounce glass, then leave it for a while. Stare at it, smell it, swirl it and enjoy the moment, because that's all it is—a single moment in time.

Wine by Design

It doesn't matter if the glass is half empty or half full.
There is clearly room for more wine.
Anonymous

The one thing you don't want to do is give the almighty wine glass and its contents power over you. You don't want to give it inflated value by looking forward to it. Instead, treat it as you would test drive a new vehicle. You sense what you want to get out of the drive, but you need time to enjoy the car and maybe the scenery. This is a chance to try something other than your favourite chardonnay, perhaps a lovely pinot noir.

There it is, sitting in front of you. It's only a glass of wine. Make the moment not about the wine but about the person you are with—and you should be with someone, rather than alone, especially if you tended to drink alone before taking control. Remember how important it is to implement change without allowing old habits back into your life.

If you find yourself focusing too much on the wine in the glass, you are glorifying the moment and taking it out of proportion. You are placing a spotlight on you and the wine. This could be extremely counterproductive, taking you back to that ugly, hairy little beast. Remember him?

Be assured that you are now in control. Sip your wine and take note of the time. Savour it, make it last and enjoy the person you chose to share this time with.

I found it helpful to change some of the smaller habits I'd built around drinking wine. I used to carry my glass with me as I moved around the house. I could be cooking dinner in the kitchen, folding laundry in the laundry room or working at my computer in the office. Lo and behold, my wine glass would follow me.

I was well aware when my wine glass became what I considered half-empty. When the wine reached the base of the glass, I felt I needed to refill to the half-full point. This left me without limits, and my consumption was difficult to measure or track. Now when I pour a glass, I'll take a small sip and leave it on the counter. I come to the glass, rather than having the glass glued to my hand. If I refill, I do so only after having two eight-ounce glasses of water over at least thirty minutes. After drinking the water, I often no longer want that second glass of wine. I've found that if you wait twenty minutes after having a drink, you'll feel like you've already had another, so why not wait? It's just like eating. If you wait ten minutes before going back for seconds, chances are you won't, because your brain has had the chance to tell your stomach it's full.

You may be asking, Why water? What about other non-alcoholic beverages with my glass of wine? Water is as pure and simple as it gets. No sugar added, and a healthy alternative to other beverages. Check the label of any alternative. If you don't find it overloaded with sugar or sodium, you'll find artificial sweeteners and other chemicals. Many of these additives are addictive. It is best to stick with the cleansing effects of good old Mother Nature.

Whether I have wine or not, I like to have tea in the evening about an hour or two before bed. My favourite is rooibis, and it's naturally caffeine-free. Caffeine-free is different from decaffeinated. The tea has not gone through any chemical process to remove caffeine because it has none. Rooibis is known for its antioxidant properties, high mineral content and other health benefits. One woman I spoke to suffered from bouts of insomnia. Her doctor prescribed sleeping pills, but while travelling on vacation, she discovered rooibis tea. "Once I tried it, there was no turning back. I have one or two cups a couple of hours before bed every night and have no trouble sleeping. I may have to get up to go to the bathroom, but I fall back to sleep without a problem. I am completely off the sleeping pills."

Baby Steps

1. Take a good look at the forthcoming week. Decide which days you know for sure you will not drink. Create an *I Will Not Drink* icon for your calendar as a reminder.
2. Steer clear of creating a new wine habit or routine. Keep mixing up the off and on days in the weeks to come, keeping within your limit when you do drink.
3. Make a pact with yourself not to drink wine at every event. Offer to be the designated driver instead.

When you do decide to enjoy wine:

1. Do not carry the glass around. Leave it in one place.
2. Sip and savour.
3. Stick to the standard pour of five ounces.
4. Make one glass last at least an hour.
5. Do not add to the glass unless it's empty and you've consumed two eight-ounce glasses of water.
6. Make a cup of caffeine-free tea before considering another glass of wine.
7. Do not drink alone.
8. Once happy hour is done, so is the wine. I'm not saying to guzzle what's left in the glass if the hour is up. Just don't pour more wine past happy hour.
9. Keep a water pitcher available and drink water before, during, in between and after wine.
10. Consider a wine spritzer: 3 ounces of wine and the rest club soda on ice. A word of caution: sometimes it's easy to lose track of how much wine you pour in a spritzer. Be sure to measure 3 to 4 ounces and keep an eye on the contents of the wine bottle. The intent is less alcohol.

In chapter one I mentioned a woman who had a take-it-or-leave-it mindset about drinking wine. That woman, whom you may have admired, envied or respected, is YOU!

Comfort Journal Prompt

Warm-Up Activity

Close your eyes and imagine you are walking along the shoreline of your favourite beach. You come across a bottle bobbing in the water. A wave delivers it to your feet. You notice a scroll in the bottle. You take the cork out and gently shake the bottle upside down, and the scroll falls into your hand. You unravel it, only to find it blank. You sit on the sand and write on the scroll. When you finish, you put the scroll back in the bottle, cork it and toss it into the ocean as far as you can.

What emotions reveal themselves to you? How does your body feel? Is it tense around your shoulders and neck? Is there tightness in your stomach? Breathe deeply into any tense areas. Hold the breath for three seconds, then release the tension as you exhale.

Comfort Journal Entry

Write what you wrote on the scroll. Who was it to? What was your message? How did it feel to write the message, to toss the bottle back into the ocean? What did it make you think about?

CHAPTER SEVEN

Social Lubrication

Why Limit Happy to an Hour?
W. C. Fields

Have you ever wondered why you do it? Why you drink wine in the first place? Here's what wine used to do for me, which is why I drank it and sometimes wish I hadn't. Under the influence of wine, I felt sexy, smart, flashy, friendly, kind, tolerant, brave, congenial, uninhibited, beautiful and transformed. And for some reason, I could suddenly sing like Lady Gaga!

Wine could also make me feel aggressive, argumentative, devastated, unworthy, ashamed, embarrassed, helpless, broken, naked, stupid and vulnerable. Where did it change me from happy and mellow to wallowing in self-pity?

For most of us, there is a fine line between how we feel following our glasses of wine and how we behave. You've heard the phrase "happy drunk," but what does it mean? Some people go quickly from mellow to weepy and sad, or to belligerent and argumentative, when they drink.

Cassie shared her story with me in the hope of saving other young women from the embarrassment she experienced at a club with friends. She called her story "Open Mouth, Insert Wine."

On a typical Saturday night, I met a couple of girl-friends at our usual club in the city for a few drinks. My week at work had been particularly stressful, as a newer coworker had been brown-nosing for a senior sales position we had both applied for. The office was non-union, and seniority meant nothing. The company had a strong work ethic strictly based on performance and potential. I knew I had made huge contributions. I had been with this employer longer than she had, and had brought several clients to the business. Yet she got the position. It almost ruined me. That Saturday night, I prepared myself to drink for the sake of drinking and to repair my deflated ego, along with my sense of unworthiness.

About four drinks into the evening, while sitting at the bar, I felt a tap on my shoulder. There she stood, smiling down at me, the girl who got the job I'd desperately wanted! Everything appeared in slow motion. Her lips began to move but I didn't hear her speak. Then she leaned in toward me. With her mouth close to my ear, I felt her words flow through the warmth of her breath. As I tried to mute her voice, I heard her say, "I hope there are no hard feelings. I know how badly you wanted the position. So did I."

I wasn't sure whether to slap her silly or to flee the scene. I did what I thought would have the most impact. I stood up slowly, turned to face her and shouted, "You may have the job now, but we'll see how long you last." The moment the words left my lips, I regretted them. My friends looked at me with distaste, wondering who I'd suddenly become. It wasn't in my nature to be outwardly cruel and aggressive. The room started to spin, and in my drunken state I sat back down, painting a smug look on my face to cover my remorse. I had completely undermined her ability, in public, and had embarrassed us both. I still can't recall her disappearing into the crowd afterward.

At work the following Monday, she deliberately avoided me. I regretted my comment and had to swallow my pride. I desperately wanted to make amends. I knew the drinks had brought out the worst in me. When the opportunity presented itself, I found her in the staff room, alone. Choking back my pride and my shame, I apologized. "I just want you to know that I didn't mean what I said Saturday night. I had had way too much to drink. Really, I know you'll do a great job. Congratulations."

Unfortunately, that did not save me from the guilt or remorse I was feeling. She didn't make eye contact and acted as though she was alone in the room. Then she turned and, standing slightly taller, walked out. I ended up leaving the company. It just became too difficult to go to work every day with such strong feelings of regret.

Why do women drink to the point of such negativity when many of us already beat ourselves up for not being smart enough, pretty enough, good enough or worthy enough? Wine can act as a stress reliever, icebreaker, meal enhancer, connector and motivator—and it can strip, depress, devastate and destroy us if we over-consume.

The online dictionary defines social lubrication as "liquor of any form that induces intoxication . . . leading to outgoing and gregarious behavior." Hmm, makes me think of weddings.

I was recently invited to a wedding at an all-inclusive resort in Mexico. A brilliant move on the part of the young couple, as the alcoholic beverages were part of a package deal that kept the wedding costs to a minimum. However, with the free flow of beverages came the socially lubricated out of their proverbial closets. As I watched young men stripping their shirts off Chippendale-style on the dance floor, I thought, good thing women don't behave this way while intoxicated. Of course, women do things too under the influence.

At another wedding, I watched a woman bump and grind with the groom of her close friend. I'm guessing they no longer consider themselves close friends.

Not only are wedding planners getting smarter about where families put their wedding dollars, but couples are thinking twice about their friends partying at their expense. Many couples head for all-inclusives, or forgo the open bar, to keep costs down. This way they can put their money to a more meaningful purpose, like purchasing a home.

It doesn't matter if it's a wedding, bridal shower or birthday celebration. When you become socially lubricated, you risk being that person everyone remembers—and not in a "I'd like to hire you for my Fortune 500 company" kind of way.

Eat, Drink, Dance

What can you do to enjoy an event without overdrinking?

- Dance! That's right. Just dance the night away. Dancing helps you unload stress, feel sexy, flirt with the guy who doesn't have a significant other and shake what your momma gave you. Dance and release, then dance some more, and you'll wake up feeling reborn. Well, some of us middle-aged folks may feel a little stiff, but definitely better than the booty-shaker on the table.

- Sure, you may find yourself thirsty after all that dancing, but before you grab that glass of chardonnay, replenish and rejuvenate your body with a beautiful, fresh, crystal clear glass of water dressed up with a lemon wedge! You won't regret it. You'll awaken without feeling any of those nasty side effects known as a hangover.

Enjoy the wonderful food that goes with special events. Glorious, delicious food slows the process of alcohol entering the blood stream. Remember the hairy beast standing on my island in the kitchen? Eat, drink water, dance your ankles off, cuz he's going down!

Comfort Journal Prompt

Warm-Up Activity

Think about someone you recall having a negative experience from excessive drinking. What did you observe and think at the time? What are you thinking and feeling now? What negative experiences have you had, if any? Reflect upon these, paying particular attention to your gut. Breathe deeply and release what no longer serves you.

Comfort Journal Entry

Write about how drinking wine makes you feel? Why do you think you do it, or overdo it, at times? How many glasses of wine does it take to get you to the fine line between a relaxed and happy state and an undesirable one? How do you want wine to make you feel? What side of the line do you want to be on?

———————

CHAPTER EIGHT

Fishbowl Margaritas

Everything in moderation, including moderation.
Oscar Wilde

B ack in the day when I enjoyed cocktails, my husband and I were taken to the land of the best margaritas ever. We were vacationing in San Diego and went on a bus tour to a small town. As we strolled through a colourful market, I was attracted to the brassy mariachi music in the distance. "Do you hear that?" I asked my husband. He stopped and nodded.

We found the source of the music, a charming Mexican restaurant with fajitas sizzling in cast iron pans. An old man with a toothless grin led us to a table looking out onto the lively market.

A multicoloured mural, depicting a time long past when indigenous people worked the land, spanned the entire length of one wall. Gazing around the crowded room, I noticed the tables and chairs. All were hand painted with intricate designs embedded with tiny mosaic tiles in loud hues of red, orange, green and yellow, found only in Mexico—or in a restaurant like this one.

A young woman with dark hair piled high on her head greeted us with a wide, pearly smile. "Our specials today are the lime margarita and chicken fajita." I nodded without hesitation and my husband ordered "Two fajitas, one lime margarita and una cerveza, por favor." The server replied, "Si, señor, ya pronto," and disappeared into the hum of the crowd.

This happened to be the place with the claim to fame of margaritas in all flavours. When the margarita arrived, I felt happy and slightly embarrassed. It was served in an actual fishbowl. I envisioned little fish donning sombreros, bopping the Mexican hat dance and partying in my drink. My husband raised an eyebrow, paused and said, "We're on vacation. Enjoy!" Enjoy I did. It was the best margarita I had ever tasted, so much so that when the food was taking so long, I ordered another.

I noticed couples with the same drink, except that they were sharing, each with a straw. I brushed it off. I was extremely thirsty and needed something while waiting for our food.

The day just seemed to get better after that. Everything looked splendid, and I could still hear the mariachi music playing. Back on the tour bus, my husband took his seat and let out a huge sigh of relief. Little did I know that I'd been leaning on him for support the entire time, and stumbling over his feet.

The Moderation Glass

I've noticed that, like the fishbowl margarita glass, wine glasses have morphed in size. I have a beautiful set of wine glasses the size of soup bowls. They seemed like a good purchase at the time, but I'd be embarrassed to use them now, and they take up valuable space. I could probably get away with using them for margaritas, if I still drank them. I suppose I could make them into candleholders or terrariums and sell them at a craft fair. One thing is certain: I won't be using them for wine.

Visit any store that sells wine glasses and you're likely to find many the size of water tumblers. I think this is how the stemless wine glass was invented. When wine glasses started looking like tumblers with stems, someone got smart, removed the stem and continued to call it a wine glass. You can pour wine to the brim, much like water, yet it doesn't look like an over-pour.

My conclusion? The size of our wine glass contributes to our wine consumption. We no longer need to be concerned about over-pouring because no one knows how much a particular glass holds, or how much is reasonable. We appear to be having a glass when in fact we are having a two-in-one glass. According to low-risk alcohol-drinking guidelines, a glass of wine measures about five ounces. Two or three glasses of wine at a party, where the pouring is free-flow and probably increasing over the evening, are more like four or six glasses. No wonder people don't feel well the morning after.

I know of a few restaurant chains that offer the choice of a 6- or 9-ounce glass of wine. A 750 ml bottle holds about 25 fluid ounces. This means that if you were to consume two 9-ounce glasses of wine, you'd be one 7-ounce glass away from drinking an entire bottle! It's a mental game and it's easy to play. Trouble is, we don't do the math. Not before the drinks, not during the drinks and certainly not after.

A study at Cornell University showed that not only does the size of the glass affect how much you pour into it, but the shape does as well. The three researchers claimed that the wider the glass, the more you end up pouring. If this isn't bad enough, the same study showed that if you hold the glass while pouring, you are likely to pour more wine. One of the researchers said, "People have trouble assessing volumes. . . . They tend to focus more on the vertical than the horizontal measures. That's why people tend to drink less when they drink from a narrow glass, because they think they're pouring more." Definitely a consideration for the red wine drinker, is it not?

Of course, not all alcohol is created equal. This book is about wine, with some exceptions. Even with wine, you will find differences in the alcohol content from bottle to bottle, and you should consider this when you decide your limit.

Recently, I came across the moderation wine glass. This cutesy wine glass has ounces marked on the side. Granted, a wine glass that looks like a measuring cup may take the "sexy" out of wine drinking. However, you do need to understand moderation. One definition is "being within reasonable limits: not excessive or extreme," while another is "an avoidance of extremes in one's actions, beliefs, or habits." Ah, there lies the key word, *habit*. Notice that it isn't *addiction* or *dependency*. Moderation in relation to wine means that if you are in the habit of drinking wine on a regular basis, then do so within reasonable limits, not excessive. This is drinking wine in moderation. This is drinking wine within your comfort zone.

When I think of moderation, I think of my friend Janice, who tried the tips and strategies I recommend and turned her life around.

My relationship with wine began in my late thirties. I was like any other young mom, working, raising kids and juggling domestic duties. I was also dealing with my aging and ailing parents, and my husband travelled a lot on business. A glass or two every evening kept me company and helped me cope with the anxieties that come from work, parenting and life's challenges.

Fast forward twenty years. Those two glasses of wine eventually led to a bottle every day, and often more on weekends. Consequently, I had been feeling somewhat distressed and was waking up each day feeling completely run down. I knew instinctively it was the wine.

During this time, my daughter was getting married. She came to me one day and said, "Mom, I need you to promise me you won't get drunk at the wedding. You're not the same person when that happens, and it happens a lot. Please don't embarrass me. Please, Mom, promise me?"

I knew she had reason for concern, but I was taken aback. My churning stomach began to rise in my throat. Forcing myself to swallow the disgrace and blinking back tears, I faked a smile. "Of course I promise." I nodded and agreed to make her proud. She hugged me, reassured, yet the sting of her comment made me realize that my impulsive relationship with wine caused her concern, anxiety and embarrassment. This jolt was enough for me to make positive changes.

I now limit myself to one or two glasses per day, weekends included, no exceptions. My daughter became my inspiration, while I became determined to wean myself back to two glasses. I only wish I'd done it sooner.

Katie Kelly Bell of Forbes.com said it well. "We all intuitively know the difference between moderate and not moderate. Alcohol, as anyone who has been affected by alcoholism will tell you, has a dark side; there should be no shame in your enjoyment. At its heart the libation is meant to be a shared experience, a tonic to celebrate food, gathering and togetherness ... of course, *in moderation.*"

By our very nature, women are intuitive and know that, for many of us, a change in our wine-drinking behaviour is necessary. Like Janice, who was well aware of the dark side of wine, many women told me they wanted practical, realistic strategies to help them get through a weeknight with less, or none. When I asked what stopped them from cutting back, they said that although they believed they could control their consumption, it would take effort and commitment and they were already completely spent.

Making the decision to moderate your drinking usually results from some concern about your wine consumption, its effect on your mind, body and spirit, as well as on your relationships and career. Although you show up for work every day, do your job and never take a day off because of a hangover, you sense that something isn't right. You don't drink in the morning or during the day, yet you return home each evening and start pouring. A glass while you cook, a glass while you eat, a glass while you clean up, and so it goes. You want to break free from the pattern, get off the merry-go-round and reclaim your power.

Is it possible to get control of your wine consumption? Absolutely! The real question is, how badly do you want to reclaim your power? Accepting your comfort-zone limit of one or two glasses per day can be both self-fulfilling and liberating. First, though, you need to work within that reasonable limit.

Comfort Journal Prompt

Warm-Up Activity

Imagine yourself ten years from now continuing to drink wine without limits. Has anything changed? How do you look? How do you feel deep inside? Do you have a message for your future self? What would you say to this future you if given a chance?

Comfort Journal Entry

Now imagine yourself ten years from now having succeeded in drinking wine in moderation. Write a letter to yourself. What would you say to this future new you?

CHAPTER NINE

Comfort Friends Forever

There comes a time in the day when no matter
what the question is, the answer is always wine.
Anonymous

Y ou now have some ongoing, workable tips and strategies
in place. In this chapter, I present the CFF system—your
Comfort Friend Forever.

When I was a teacher, librarian and mentor, colleagues came
to my office on many occasions to share their frustrations, sometimes about the job, but most often simply to vent life's challenges. Cynthia became alarmed when she noticed her wine consumption climbing over a six-month period. Her three-year-old
twins, Zack and Zoe, were bundles of pure energy. Although
Cynthia adored her children, she looked forward to the end of
each day, kids tucked safely in bed, when she could sip her glasses
of wine and relax.

As a working mom, Cynthia noticed that getting up in the
morning was becoming increasingly difficult. She came to me one
day after work, looking completely overwhelmed, and told me,

"I find myself frustrated and depleted before the day even gets started. I'm snapping at the kids and my husband more often."

When her husband questioned the change he'd noticed in her behaviour, Cynthia broke down and told him, "I just need a break! I'm drinking too much wine and I feel like crap. I thought wine would help. It's not."

Cynthia's husband offered support but didn't know how to help, so he recommended she see her doctor. "A genuine fear shook through me at the thought of telling my doctor I was drinking wine every night to relax. I didn't want my doctor to have a bad opinion of me, or cast me off as some loser with a drinking problem, but I also didn't feel I fit the profile of the classic alcoholic, whatever that is."

Determined to take this on, Cynthia called her best friend, Lana. Lana also enjoyed her glasses of wine each night after her kids were in bed. After hearing Cynthia's fears, Lana consoled her: "Oh Cynthia, you don't need a doctor. We need a girls' night out. How about next Thursday?" Cynthia agreed. The two women met and proceeded to drink, laugh, drink, console and drink some more. Unfortunately, this was not the solution Cynthia was searching for.

The next morning, feeling worse than most days, Cynthia made a doctor appointment. Surprisingly, her doctor did not see wine as the problem. Rather, she suggested Cynthia change her evening routine. She thought that, although Cynthia often drank, she simply needed something rewarding and inspiring outside the home, away from her family.

Cynthia decided to join an evening yoga class. "I met Elaine and we hit it off right away. With her extensive background in health and fitness, I trusted her. It wasn't long before I told her about my relationship with wine."

One day after yoga class, Elaine asked Cynthia, "Is the yoga making a difference?" Cynthia told me, "Yoga did make a positive difference, and so did Elaine. I had a new, healthy activity, a couple of evenings a week outside the house, and I made a new friend."

For Cynthia, finding her new comfort friend was as simple as changing routines a couple of nights a week. Her CFF supported her new intention to cut back on her wine intake, as well as to do something healthy and gratifying.

Here are some opportunities to make new friends:

- Sign up for a craft class, such as pottery, painting, scrapbooking, weaving, quilting, knitting, flower arranging, jewelry-making or calligraphy.

- Enroll in a competitive sport like rowing, curling, hockey, basketball, baseball, soccer or volleyball.

- Try something new like snowshoeing, snowboarding or skiing in winter, and paddle boarding, sailing, canoeing or swimming in the summer.

- Join a fitness club and try weight training, spinning or the various cardio classes.

- Join a boot camp or cycling group, or try a martial art such as karate or tai chi.

- Start a book club, perhaps meeting up at a coffee shop. Invite two of your friends and ask each of them to invite two people you don't know.

- Start a walking club, doing the same as with the book club. Visit different areas in nature.

It all depends on what you enjoy doing besides drinking wine. Comfort friends don't appear out of nowhere. It's when change occurs that opportunity presents itself. The only one who can create change in your wine routine is you, and when you do, chances are you'll make new friends.

There were two people I knew *not* to consider as my comfort friend: my husband and my best friend. Why? Because these are people I'm very close to. My husband is one of my best friends. In no way should he be in control of my wine drinking. Role model yes, control no. For him to be in control would only create stress in our relationship. I would likely hold him accountable for my actions rather than owning the responsibility myself.

Best friends are the friends who stand by you through bad hair days, risky adventures and bad dates. They may fall into the Thelma and Louise type of friendship. You know, the ones you'd drive off a cliff with. But using your best friend as your comfort friend would be like taking one another down a rabbit hole.

The cast of *Cougar Town* guzzles wine on such a regular basis that when the character Jules decides to abstain for a few days, her best friend tells her, "Nothing could ever make me stop loving you, except you not drinking."

Best friends know when they should tell one another to stop, but it would likely come out something like this: "We don't want to have another drink, right? Okay, we do." Giggle, giggle, and then come the excuses: "We deserve it, we work hard. But just one, okay?"

I'm assuming here that you and your best friend drink wine in much the same way. And both of you have good intentions. But you'll end up enabling one another rather than supporting each other not to have that one more glass. Definitely, continue to share your successes with your best friend, and be there to listen to hers. That's what best friends do. But if you and your best friend have the same drinking tendency, don't under any circumstances put yourselves in the position of supporting one another as a comfort friend. If you do, you'll risk driving off that cliff and losing a best friend along the way, forever.

Even with the best of intentions, we sometimes let ego dictate pleasure over common sense. Your comfort friend should be someone you trust. She should also be someone who doesn't have the same wine tendencies as you and who supports your interest in healthier activities.

The following list of excuses may be helpful when you want just one more glass. Keep it handy on your smart phone and add to it as circumstances arise. When you are presented with a challenging situation and begin talking yourself into one more glass, read the excuses. If it's a new one-liner, add it to the list. Finding your excuse on the list, or creating a new one to add, makes you more aware, in effect helping you not have one more glass. If all else fails, call your CFF.

Just One More Glass

I'm going to have just one more glass because . . .

- I don't have to drive.
- It's been such a brutal week.
- I have the night off from kids or _____
- I don't have to work tomorrow.
- I want to celebrate.
- I need to celebrate.
- I'm celebrating _____
- I feel like it.

- I can't deal with him/her.
- I'm not relaxed yet.
- I deserve it.
- I'm depressed.
- I need an extra boost.

Think of this as your personal list of excuses, a form of wining and wallowing in self-pity, none of which serves any purpose. Excuses will only hold you back from reclaiming your power. They are your body's way of telling your mind what it wants. Your body does this because it's used to getting its way. You are not your body. You are *you*. Your body just houses your spirit and soul. *You* are the one that gets to decide what your body needs and deserves, not the other way around.

One Giant Leap for Womankind

Women need to bring their wine drinking out of the closet, take a giant leap forward and support one another through the journey to controlled drinking. By the word *controlled* I mean drinking in moderation. The old saying "There is strength in numbers" is especially true here. In the past, too many women did not seek help because they believed they were completely and utterly alone.

In many support groups of chronic alcoholics, members share similar pain and struggles. Your Comfort Friend Forever, or CFF, should *not* be one of those people. She should *not* have a wine habit. A CFF puts your best interests before a glass of wine and has no problem telling you straight, though in a positive light, what you need to hear. She should be readily available to you and able to talk you out of one more glass, not because she has been there, but more importantly because she hasn't. She has used healthier strategies to get through a hectic day than drinking wine and can therefore be an excellent confidant.

Your comfort friend supports you without making you feel bad about yourself. She would never say anything like, "I don't understand you. Look at what you're doing to your body, your relationship, your family." Your comfort friend is your encourager, cheerleader, confidant and biggest fan—and she believes in you. She focuses on what you *are* doing to change, not on what you *were* doing to get where you are.

Your CFF may be someone you would least expect, or someone you've always wanted to get to know better. You may need to invest in a life coach, mentor or counsellor to give you the help you'll need. Whoever she is, she should have your best interests in mind. It takes time to develop a relationship like this. That's okay because it will be worth it. *You* are worth it.

Make a promise to yourself each week. What exactly can you and will you do to interrupt your wine routine? Be sure to stay away from any new routine involving alcohol. Focus instead on the new activity. Include your comfort friend in your promise and write it down. It's not enough to state that you'll cut back by going to dance class. You need to be specific and focus on what you will do instead of drinking wine. Here's an example:

My Promise

- This week, I promise to work on my tai chi routine every day right after work.
- I also promise to meet with my CFF on Tuesday and Thursday at 7 p.m. to practise our tai chi routine.
- I will stick to this by having my change of clothes ready when I get home after work.

■ I will follow my session with a tall cleansing glass of lemon water.

Earlier in this book, you discovered the one- to two-glass limit. While your promise confirms this reality, it does not focus on it. By this I mean, in placing your attention on the new activity (tai chi), you are shifting your thoughts (from wine to tai chi) and changing your routine and behaviour. Your promise has the potential to create a balanced lifestyle that includes enjoying wine, in moderation, along with other healthy behaviours.

Comfort Journal Prompt

Warm-Up Activity

Close your eyes and go back to a time when you were engaged in an activity that inspired you. What were you doing? How did it feel? Is it something you can do now? What other activities fulfill a passion within you? Think about what might refocus your thoughts and behaviours.

Comfort Journal Entry

Make your promise and write it in your journal. Be sure to include answers to the following questions: What activity will I do? When will I practise it? How will I set myself up for success so that I will stick to my promise?

Sign your promise. Read it out loud. Say it in the mirror. Say it to your CFF. Mean it. Stick to it!

CHAPTER TEN

Weed Your Social Garden

Wine makes daily living easier, less hurried,
with fewer tensions and more tolerance.
Benjamin Franklin

Our social circles are built upon commonalities, such as work, activities or kids the same age. Yet from time to time, it may be necessary to unfriend someone within a group, or possibly the entire group, to respect your personal boundaries. I call this "weeding your social garden." I'm not implying that some people are like weeds, needing to be plucked and tossed aside. Rather, I want you to focus on your relationships and notice the impact some people have on your life. Consider carefully those you would call true friends. By examining the reasons for your social connections, you can determine the difference between true friends and those who don't have your best interests in mind.

A young woman I know, Diane, made the bold decision to start weeding when she realized her life was not going to change for the better until she took action. Diane graduated from high school with a strongly connected group of about twelve young men and women. Although individual interests and career goals varied, the group was tightly knit, having been part of their high school athletic club.

Many left for universities outside their hometown but stayed connected via social media and reunited on their visits home. Those who remained in town, however, continued to meet at a local club every Saturday night and sometimes on Wednesdays. It was a big party scene with an outrageous amount of drinking.

Diane and her friend Jolene spent a lot of time on the dance floor, with or without one of the guys. Many of the guys would initiate games involving pints of beer followed by shots of vodka, and Jolene, unfortunately, would often get involved. When she wasn't dancing, Diane would watch the group shift from a happy bunch of young people to a pack of obnoxious adolescents. When Jolene crossed the line and became drunk, she would dare Diane to join in. This repeated itself on many occasions. Every time Diane refused, Jolene would go a little further, trying to draw her in. "C'mon, Diane, you know you want to." Diane didn't want to, and she couldn't understand why Jolene tried to force this upon her.

One Wednesday night, the drinking game got underway as usual and Jolene started making her usual pleas. "C'mon, Diane, if you're my friend you'll join me. I'll buy the drinks."

This time Diane had a plan. "As soon as Jolene started begging, I got up and walked out. I was so tired of the club scene and knew I couldn't reason with Jolene. I couldn't imagine myself in a few years, stuck in the past."

Jolene called Diane the next day. "Why did you leave me there? What kind of friend does that?"

With as much courage as she could muster, Diane replied, "What kind of friend doesn't respect the other's wishes?"

Diane knew she wanted nothing to do with this excessive drinking and it was time to take action. She also knew it wasn't going to be easy, living in a small town with many friends away at university. She explained to me, "I knew that if I continued going to the club, I'd eventually cave in and take part in the drinking, making me like everyone else in that group. It's not that I thought I was better than them, just that I no longer wanted to spend my free time in meaningless behaviour."

Jolene kept calling Diane, trying to convince her to go to the club. It took every bit of courage to finally confront Jolene with honesty. "I knew that being honest would help me confront my fear of ending up lonely, as well as confirm my social boundaries. When I told Jolene I wasn't interested in the club scene anymore, she completely disconnected from me. It was hard at first, because I considered her a friend, but to this day I have no regrets."

Ten years later, Diane has kept in contact with a few of the girls, some of whom had left town for university. When the ten-year high school reunion came up, Diane and a few others went together. Not surprisingly, the usual club group sat together, cajoling one another in an exaggerated manner.

Diane and the women she came with mingled through the groups, exchanging predictable conversation. "Great to see you. You look fantastic. Is that a wedding ring on your finger? How many kids?" Passing by the bar, she noticed Jolene with a few of the guys ordering shots.

Diane said a quick hello and kept moving. "I couldn't even make eye contact with her. Part of me was afraid she would try to befriend me again, and seeing her only made me realize I'd made the right decision all those years ago." As Diane politely passed them by, she let go of the past.

When you weed your social garden, you take a bold step forward, with no need to look back. Most people aren't deliberately condescending or mean. They're just unaware of the connection between their behaviour and their friendships. However, there will always be those people who *are* aware and deliberately use you. Let's face it. Excessive drinking is way more acceptable in a group. Everyone who's doing it looks more normal than you sitting on a bar stool drinking cranberry soda.

The drinking scene in today's pop culture offers the potential for idealized friendships. Not taking part in the partying scene may leave you feeling undesirable, but looking beyond those types of social circles can lead you to find true friendships built on the right foundation.

Opportunities for long, positive friendships often present themselves when we engage in activities with others. However, not all of these friendships end up being of the lasting kind. That's okay. My best and closest relationships are those that have survived the test of time and circumstance, and they have become stronger for it. More importantly, while my closest friends and I have a lot in common, we respect our differences. We are honest with each other and confide anything, confident that it will stay put. We would come to each other's aid in a heartbeat, unconditionally. However, when a friendship becomes one-sided, as in the case of Diane and Jolene, it's time to let it go. Had Jolene been sensitive and caring to Diane, she would never have expected Diane to take the dare, as that would have crossed personal boundaries. This friendship was built on one person, Diane, being the giver, and the other, Jolene, being the taker.

Breaking routines and rituals with friends and acquaintances is difficult, but finding new, healthier friendships will support your wellness. It's never too late to make a lasting, genuine friendship.

Avoid the Anchors

Although I believe that, in general, women share a bond, there are some who use others for their own benefit. I call these women "anchors." Let me be clear about what an anchor is. An anchor is a person who seeks attention from others to meet her own needs. The anchor involved in excessive drinking desperately needs the company of others to look and feel normal. She feels threatened by anyone not willing to go along, and will go to great lengths to get them to do so.

Perhaps you want to break free from a group of women who engage in habitual behaviours that you know will involve drinking too much wine. Begin by breaking the pattern a little at a time. Plan an alternative event that affords you the opportunity to make new friends, like the activities you explored in the last chapter—a dance class, craft studio, volunteer organization, anything that makes you feel good and involves others. This will guide you away from the social circle and circumstances you want to avoid.

Don't allow others to become your anchor. Most anchors are looking for company—someone to go down with them to the depths of despair. After all, misery loves company, doesn't it? Think of the anchor as misery desperately needing your company. The only time an anchor makes an effort to do what you want is when she sees something in it for herself. You cannot change her, nor should you try. You'll only end up sinking deeper into that dark place, alone and at your own expense.

Anchors need support and guidance beyond what you, as a friend, can perhaps offer. Remaining friends while continuing to behave in ways that are not your own creates a toxic relationship and usually ends badly. You have the ability to tap into your inner wisdom. Trust what is right for you and watch rewarding changes come your way.

Choosing Soothers

Following the birth of her second child, Sally joined a social circle of women like herself who loved wine and connecting with one another on mommy playdates that included their children. The women met twice a month to share the trials and tribulations of childbearing, childrearing and everything in between. These get-togethers, where they enjoyed glasses of wine while children played underfoot, were a source of mommy-bonding, laughter and relief.

When Sally noted her drinking throughout the week and even more on the weekend, she questioned whether she was drinking too much. Not believing she quite fit the definition of alcoholic, she decided to try cutting back. Here is Sally's story:

> Although I never drank while pregnant, I really looked forward to the day I could go back to it. After my first pregnancy, I found that having a glass of wine seemed to mellow me out and keep me grounded. What I hadn't noticed was that I had started drinking every day, especially once the baby started sleeping through the night.
>
> I wasn't what I considered to be a normal drinker. I had attempted to drink in moderation several times and would eventually find myself pouring more to make up for lost time. I just wanted it too much at the end of each day, never satisfied with one or even two glasses and unable to take it or leave it like many of my friends. I decided that for me the best course of action was to quit. It didn't happen overnight, and

I did relapse several times. Now, however, there is no turning back.

At first I was scared of a lot of things, like being noticed at social events, or worse, people finding me boring. I also worried about the gossip and losing friends, not to mention what I would do instead of drink. I started journaling, tracking my cravings and replacing happy hour with other activities. I filled my evenings spending time with my baby and husband, good books and much-needed sleep.

I agonized over the mommy playdates and whether I should keep going. I decided not to go, realizing that they might be counterproductive to quitting. Fortunately, many of the women understood and have stayed in touch. Some of us go to dance class together or meet for tea or coffee, kids in tow. A few members, though, were a little miffed. I can't do anything about that, and I won't apologize for doing what's in my best interests and my family's.

The other night I was putting my eight-month-old to bed. As I stroked her back, she squirmed and wriggled, trying to fight off the sandman. While she sucked intensely on her soother, her eyes became heavy. The soother slid from her tiny lips and I watched her drift off to baby dreamland. The old Sally would have missed that moment. Today, I'm here for my family, and I'm a better mom and person for having taken this step.

Sally made the decision to weed her social garden by no longer attending the mommy playdates. She easily maintained her friendships with some of the women in the group through other activities they enjoyed. Sally decided that the best course of action for her was to quit drinking altogether. She hasn't looked back. Sally used many of the steps and strategies in this book, including the journal prompts, to keep her on track, along with professional support.

For some of us, quitting completely may be best. Only you can honestly determine that. Although I have been able to take it or leave it, I recognize that there are many women who struggle to keep drinking off their minds. If you spend a lot of time thinking about whether wine is a problem, perhaps it is. If wine is interfering with the quality of your life, and you've made several unsuccessful attempts to moderate it, perhaps you should consider quitting, as Sally boldly did.

Wherever this book finds you, it is my sincere hope that it guides you to make the decision that is best for you. In no way do I advocate that everyone can drink in moderation. Each of us needs to decide what is best for us, and I believe we can determine that by tapping into our inner wisdom. My father once said, "All you need to get through this is within you." That includes the answer to the question whether you should drink in moderation or not at all.

There will always be people in this world who are unhappy and would love you to join them. The unfortunate part is that they often don't appear to be unhappy. They may be hardworking, focused on their careers and supportive. Yet all too often these women use wine and the company of friends to fill their needs. Regardless of the need they are trying to fill, the anchors will surround themselves with anyone willing to behave in the same manner.

You have the ability to transform your life by changing your wine routine and leading a healthier lifestyle. No doubt when you make the decision, you will discover who your real friends are. Your real friends will support you, back you, encourage you, cheer you on and be proud of you. They won't judge you or try to make you fail or feel guilty about your decision. Your intuition, those feelings in your gut, will guide you. And chances are, when positive changes emerge, your real friends will want to join you.

Make quality time for those you consider to be good friends. If there is wine involved, take time to enjoy it with them, within your comfort zone. Once you've weeded your social garden, you will be able to take time to smell the wine and enjoy your friends along the way.

Comfort Journal Prompt

Warm-Up Activity

Think about authentic friendship and what it means to you. Make a list of everyone you consider to be your closest friends and why. Who would support you, whether you decide to drink in moderation or not at all? Do you feel judged? Are your friendships unconditional? Are your friends givers by nature?

Comfort Journal Entry

Write a letter to one of your closest friends. Tell her how grateful you are for her friendship and what she means to you. Tell her about your decision to cut back or quit drinking wine. Tell her your concerns, fears and hopes. Thank her for her support. Imagine giving the letter only to her.

Reread your letter. How do you feel?

CHAPTER ELEVEN

The Grapevine

One not only drinks wine, one smells it, observes it,
tastes it, sips it and—one talks about it.
King Edward VII

Women today are career-minded, hardworking, caregiving survivors, thanks to their predecessors who fought hard for women's rights. Women get up every morning, empty the dishwasher, throw in a load of laundry, cook breakfast, make lunches, vacuum, dust and then head for the shower. Once kids are off to school, they head to work, where they juggle calendars, projects, assignments and meetings. An average day for a woman puts new meaning to the twenty-four-hour schedule, with parent-teacher nights, recitals and sporting events, and organizing car pools, bottle drives and bake sales. Women wipe noses and other body parts, take out the trash, fix the toilet and paint a bedroom, all the while striving for perfection. Despite all that women do, they wear an impressive smile, when anyone notices, and still look like a million bucks at the end of the day—even after an hour at boot camp. Oh yes, we've come a long way, baby.

Perhaps a slight exaggeration, the fact remains that many women are exhausted at the end of each day. There is a common thread among women today—a desire for connection, acceptance and recognition. For most women, when they share a bottle of wine, they are sharing and baring more than their souls. They are sharing their passions, their hearts, fears and dreams. Women console one another, get to the heart of every matter, feel each other's pain, and even join forces for the benefit of one who has fallen, making the bond even stronger.

Given all that women do, it's no wonder there's a tendency to self-medicate, to numb, to melt into the evening. There are myriad wines yet to be swirled, swished, tasted and swallowed, but mostly to be shared. Let's hope that in doing so, women don't find themselves on the dark side of wine.

When I told a friend, Jenna, about this book, she gasped, "This is so timely. My daughter Megan and her friends need to get their hands on this."

Megan had sent an email to her mother disclosing how terribly unbalanced she felt. Megan ended her hectic workdays with one or two glasses of wine each evening and most of a bottle at least one night a week. A hardworking, focused twenty-seven-year-old, Megan had a zest for life and usually worked hard to stick to her health, wellness and physical fitness goals.

Megan had landed a new and demanding position that overwhelmed her. She wasn't eating properly and often found herself over-consuming glasses of wine, at home alone. As a mom, Jenna felt utterly helpless and blamed herself. "I drink a glass or two of wine every day and have for many years. It's my fault Megan is drinking too much."

Not only did Jenna blame herself for Megan's decision to turn to wine, but like any concerned parent, she worried for her daughter's physical and mental well-being. "I haven't been able to sleep, I've been so worried about her. I even started searching for treatment programs online."

I suggested to Jenna that Megan try some of the tips and strategies in this book. Jenna, with Megan's permission, offered to share the email, hoping other young women might relate and learn from her experience.

> Mom, for the past month I have been pushing myself hard at work. I've wanted to do well and make good first impressions. It has taken a lot out of me, and at the end of each day I have found myself completely overwhelmed. The last thing I feel like doing is a workout. Instead, I opt to pick up a bottle of wine and enjoy the effects of total relaxation coming over me. Sometimes I'm alone, sometimes I'll have a friend over, but most times I prefer to be alone.
>
> The other day it occurred to me that drinking wine every day is accepted, convenient and takes such little effort. I've fallen into this routine for about a month now. Trouble is, it's zapping my energy. I don't feel healthy and I don't like how I feel in the morning. I'm tired before I even start my hectic workday, and this is of great concern to me.
>
> It seems that many of my friends engage in this behaviour on a regular basis. It's a wonder any of us handle our day-to-day lives. Well, we're not. I'm not.
>
> Mom, people my age are hitting the bars more frequently and regularly than ever. We all seem in search of connection, yet the drinking is disconnecting us from everything that really matters, including

ourselves. It used to be that we would meet to social-
ize, talk and laugh. Now, we meet to drink for the sake
of drinking. There was a time we looked forward to
the weekend and spending it with one another over a
drink, but that has changed into a regular daily scene
for way too many of us. Can you imagine what weekends look like now?

Just last Sunday I met a friend of mine for breakfast.
She didn't hesitate to order a glass of pinot grigio. She
told me it helps take the rough edge off the hangover
from the night before. It was only 10 a.m., Mom.

All of this has made me aware that it's time to make
some changes in my lifestyle. Please don't worry
about me, Mom. You know me. I'll be okay, I promise.
I just wanted you to know what's happening in my life.
I love you, Mom.

Megan

Jenna didn't believe that Megan was alcohol-dependent,
but she recognized that the potential was there and her daughter needed support. Jenna presented Megan with many of the
ideas from this book. A few months after our first conversation,
Jenna called to tell me that Megan's circumstances had improved.
She followed many of the tips and strategies suggested here and
decided to take the lead among her friends. In doing so she also
took charge of her life. Then Jenna added, "I'm using the strategies as well, and it's been incredibly empowering and healing. I
feel like I'm a better mom for it, and the two of us are definitely
closer."

Megan cut out drinking during the week, as did Jenna, and
encouraged two of her friends to join a dragon boat racing team.
The challenge was both physically and mentally demanding,

leaving no room for wine through the week. Megan's team met at six a.m. three days in the week and every Sunday morning. Megan discovered that not only did she feel re-energized and focused, but she was more efficient at work. More importantly, she didn't miss having wine.

When Megan connected with friends in a drinking environment, she knew ahead whether she was drinking, and if so, she planned out her drink limit. If her peers asked about it, she told them about the dragon boat racing and asked for their support.

How many other young women are falling into these daily drinking routines but, unlike Jenna's daughter, don't know who to turn to or what to do about it?

Tiptoe through the Grapevine

Women who do know who to turn to are coming out of the wine closet, spreading the word and sharing their intimate relationship with wine with other women. As a result, these women are feeling empowered and are collectively creating a women's movement focused on health, wellness and the prevention of dependency on alcohol.

Although family history can provide you with important information about the relationship others have had with alcohol, it does not destine you to develop the same tendencies. It is essential, however, to have this knowledge, as well as to be familiar with recent research. This knowledge is your power.

It is equally important to share your concerns with your doctor and to ask him or her questions regarding your personal risk factors. If you have a family history of diabetes, breast cancer or heart disease, for example, drinking beyond moderation puts you at higher risk. In fact, drinking in excess puts you at risk regardless of family history. Why increase your chances? Drinking in excess on a regular basis is like playing Russian roulette. Do you really want to pull that trigger?

Be sure your doctor is up to date on alternative methods of dealing with a daily wine habit and/or alcohol dependency. Do not allow yourself to be cast into a one-size-fits-all approach, as I once was. Be your own advocate, and be aware of all the contributing factors that surround you. Use everything in your power to understand your relationship with wine, and use it to take back control.

Have an open conversation with family members and closest friends about your plan to cut back. Educate your children, if you have them, and be a positive role model to everyone who knows you. In doing so, you will not only help others but will be creating a supportive network.

After all my alcohol-related experiences, I found the following two points central to women making healthier decisions about their relationship with wine:

1. Knowledge of family history and risk assessment in relation to wine consumption and your personal potential for disease.
2. Research and education about alcohol. Once you understand the consequences of over-consuming regularly, you will be able to make an informed decision whether to relearn to drink in moderation or quit altogether.

Many government health agencies promote the prevention and early detection of breast and other cancers, diabetes, strokes and heart disease. I have yet to see anything boldly advertising the possible consequences of alcohol abuse. Sure, you'll see signs, posters and commercials warning you not to drink alcohol while pregnant, not to drink and drive, and to support dry grads. But it's rare to come across an ad or public display about how to prevent alcohol dependency. Can you imagine this warning, like the ones on cigarette packages, on bottles of wine? "Excessive drinking has potential health hazards. Know your limit, drink within it."

Advertising, cultural trends and our own personal beliefs— "Oh, it will never happen to me"—all have a strong influence on the growing number of people becoming dependent on wine, or on alcohol in general.

Wine is never going to be banned, nor should it be. The days of prohibition are long past, and women are now keeping step with men. I believe there is a real need for education among our younger population, including what it means to drink in moderation. Boomers to millennials need to break the chain of drinking in excess and using alcohol to relax, numb or self-medicate. It's time for women to join the grapevine and raise awareness about the consequences of excessive drinking, particularly for women. This raised awareness will help prevent future generations from passing the corkscrew down the line.

Children learn from what they're exposed to—but they have choices. I read a story about twin sons who had an alcoholic father. One son became an alcoholic and the other didn't. When asked why they drank or not, they responded similarly. The alcoholic son said, "I'm an alcoholic because my dad was an alcoholic," whereas the non-alcoholic son said, "I'm not an alcoholic because my dad was an alcoholic." This story illustrates that they each had a choice to make.

If children see mom or dad abusing alcohol, there is a good chance they will grow up believing that alcohol is a way to cope in life. However, it is not inevitable that they themselves will become abusers of alcohol. They learn the behaviours and may repeat them out of not knowing or never having been taught other ways of coping with life's challenges.

Breaking the Chain

Jennifer and Jillian's story demonstrates both their courage and determination. Because their mother, considered a chronic alcoholic, had been unsuccessful at several attempts at rehabilitation, the twenty-nine-year-old twins made it their life's mission not to become alcohol dependent. Jennifer, the more outspoken of the two, shared their story.

> Our parents divorced when we were ten years old. We spent many years being passed back and forth between them while they lived reckless and chaotic lives. Our dad, a construction worker, remarried, and his wife was merciless and insanely jealous of us. Consequently, we didn't like being around either of them.
>
> Our mom, a waitress in a local pub, came home late most nights. She'd be all keyed up and would drink until she passed out. There were countless nights Jillian and I would put a pillow under Mom's head after she'd passed out, and we'd cover her with a blanket. We felt like her parent.
>
> We'd get ourselves up and have to wake her to drive us to school, and we were often late. Worse, she would often end up in the local bar before noon and

then nap past the time she was supposed to pick us up from school.

The two of us would go to the playground and wait, rain or shine. We'd lie to the teacher and our friends and say we were waiting for our mom to get off work. Sometimes it would start to get dark before she'd show up. I remember one night it had gotten so dark we could see the janitor working in one of the class-rooms, all lit up and empty. I kept thinking about all those kids, home safe, eating dinner with their fam-ilies or watching TV. It hurt so much but I refused to cry. I never wanted to upset Jillian.

That night, when Mom finally came for us, she was really quiet. It was her night off work, and I think she must have felt bad because she picked up a pizza on the way home. There was a beer and wine store next to the pizza place. While Jillian and I waited for the pizza, Mom went next door. When she came out, she was carrying a twelve pack of beer. She put the case on the floor of the passenger side and reached down to crack one open, but she caught the horror in my eyes. Fortunately, she waited until we got home and then proceeded to drink the entire case. I counted them in the morning.

Most nights when Mom was at work, we would lie awake waiting and hoping she'd get home safe and sober. We are thankful that we've always had each other and shared the fear of living day to day in con-stant neglect and uncertainty. We took nothing for granted, nor assumed anything other than the worst. We always wanted to be prepared in case something bad happened.

These were confusing and painful years for the twins. Jennifer internalized the negative influence of her mother's drinking, feeling angry and yearning for her mother's love and acceptance. It was difficult for both girls to rationalize how their mom could choose alcohol over them.

Fortunately, both twins had caring friends whose parents offered each of them a home. As teenagers, they were old enough to decide where they wanted to live, and though they would be separated, they knew this was the best option. These families offered the girls stable and loving homes, which to this day have had a positive impact.

Both girls vowed never to have a relationship with the dark side of alcohol. They had witnessed firsthand how easily a life can be consumed by its seductive influence. Jillian told her friend's mom, "I will never overindulge in alcohol because it will always remind me of how my mom chose her pints of beer over Jennifer and me. It hurts so much to know that."

Jennifer still carries the pain of a child always waiting for the love of her mother, and as an adult, continues to search for meaning in the suffering of her past. "In an effort to numb my pain, I started drinking wine every day after work. I thought of it as harmless, not like the beers and shots my mom drank."

Along with counselling, Jennifer has been using the strategies in this book to help her control her wine intake. She told me, "I love journaling and focusing on now and the future rather than my painful past. Although I did need to forgive my mom, it doesn't help me to look back anymore."

Jennifer promised Jillian that she'd cut back her wine intake, and she has kept that promise. She purchased special paper decorated with butterflies around the border and wrote a promise to her sister: *Dear Jillian, I will support my mind, body and soul, offering only nourishing food and beverages to maintain a healthy balance. I love myself and I love you.*

Jennifer put this on her fridge where she would see it every morning and read it aloud. She called me one evening to share how wonderfully things were working out for her. "I've joined a volunteer organization called Big Brothers Big Sisters, and I go right from work two days a week. Giving back has given my life new meaning. When I do get home from work, the first thing I do is eat, then make tea. Afterward, I light a candle and visualize. I have found that the desire for wine has been replaced with an inner peace that came through my daily visualization practice. Now when I have wine, it is in moderation and within my comfort zone."

Comfort Journal Prompt

Warm-Up Activity

Think about your family history or your experiences with people you know who abuse alcohol. What do you believe about their relationship with alcohol? Do you believe as they do? Do their beliefs impact you in any way? If so, how? If not, why not?

Comfort Journal Entry

Write about your beliefs regarding women's relationship with wine and how you are impacted by what you and/or others believe? What can you do to break the chain among family and/or friends?

CHAPTER TWELVE

Self-Care

Wine is one of the most civilized things in the world and one of the most natural things of the world that has been brought to the greatest perfection, and it offers a greater range for enjoyment and appreciation than, possibly, any other purely sensory thing.

Ernest Hemingway

As caregivers, women often tend to everyone else's needs before their own. While younger women juggle careers, domestic duties and the needs of young children, middle-aged women feel torn between their growing family and aging parents.

Women struggling to cope with daily challenges often overlook self-care. The occasional spa treatment may be viewed as too expensive or time-consuming or, sadly, undeserving. Yet, taking time for oneself is exactly what women need. In her book *When Mom's Happy Everyone's Happy: A Guide for Improving Self-Identity and Relationships*, Susan Dawes explains that women who set aside time for themselves often feel more fulfilled and happier than those who don't. And it doesn't matter how they spend this time, whether it be a spa treatment, shopping for shoes or taking a quiet hour with a cup of tea and a good book. The act of gifting oneself with a precious moment of time leads women to feel happier.

Intending to gift themselves, many women turn to wine as a reward, often with such comments as "I deserve it. It's been a hectic day. I'm totally stressed out. I work hard." What they are doing is creating the false belief that wine will make them feel better, recharge their battery or satisfy some burning desire. Yet nothing could be further from the truth. In reality, women are disconnecting from themselves rather than reconnecting to their inner wisdom and thus their personal power.

Educating yourself about the long-term benefits of self-care, leading to improved health and wellness, is a step toward making it happen. Self-care is not just about nutrition and exercise. It is equally about being in balance spiritually, creatively and emotionally. There should be no shame in putting yourself first, without that wine glass in hand. When you feel good, you'll be happier, and when you're happier, everyone you touch will be happier too.

It's been said time and time again that alcohol is a depressant, one that women need to steer clear of when they feel vulnerable. Yet the worst time to drink is the very time when many women do—when they feel stressed, run down and tired. This only perpetuates the problem.

Create a Master Plan for yourself. Here are some things to consider:

- If you have decided not to drink through the week, make sure you have a plan that works, such as not having wine in the house. That way, it will be easier to stick to your plan.

- When you decide to have wine, do it with intention. Delight in it. Pair it with delicious food and good company. Make it worth your while, but not in an excessive sense.

- Find a follow-up, non-alcoholic beverage to signal your body that you are done with wine for the evening. You'll be retraining your body and mind to expect something else. I make ice water with a variety of fruit as a standby. I find that my guests usually join me, as it is inviting, thirst-quenching and colourful. Don't be afraid to experiment with kiwi, pineapple, apple and strawberry, for starters.

I Am Worthy, I Am Loveable

After the pivotal moments I've shared with you, I attended a conference put on by a large self-help community of authors and public speakers. It was timely. As a lifelong learner, I immersed myself for three intense days, gathering as much information as I could. Soon after the conference, and because I was seeking ways to cut back on wine, I took the beginning steps toward transforming my life. I recognized my capacity to tap into my inner wisdom.

I read many books on spirituality and engaged in meditation, visualization, yoga and writing. I asked myself some important questions about wine. For example: Will I cut back or quit? Will I need support? Will I be able to drink in moderation? How many other women are in this situation?

Call it a spiritual awakening or an intuitive sixth sense, but I woke up Monday morning after the conference and knew what lived in my heart. That weekend, while listening to countless speakers share their wellness message, I learned a deep, dark secret about my personal beliefs. What I hold within is deeply rooted from childhood. Throughout my life, I have carried feelings of being unworthy and undeserving, along with a need to seek approval and acceptance.

From my awakening I created a framework for the steps that would lead to self-care. This became the foundation for this book, as well as my forthcoming book, *The Self-Care Solution: Ten Steps to Taking Care of You While Taking Care of Everyone Else.*

I nourished my body with healthy, whole foods and nurtured my soul using the methods and techniques I've shared here. Although I continue to enjoy wine, I do so mindfully and with intention. My body no longer tells my mind that I need it. Along my learning path, I discovered that when my reason for having a glass of wine changed, so did the routine, quantity and my ability to enjoy it within my comfort zone.

Once I got started on the self-care path, my life took a spin in an exciting new direction. Although I loved my job as a teacher-librarian, I'd reached the point of exhaustion. I deeply desired—needed, actually—to do something new and inspiring. I decided to retire from teaching, to read, study, write and serve in a new way. I continued to teach, mentor and serve those who might learn from my life experiences of self-care, and I began to see value in my purpose. I treasure my interactions with others and the lessons I've learned from them.

A woman's insight is a revealing sixth sense. It was when I clarified my purpose to serve others by sharing personal experiences that the way to do it became clear. My inner wisdom had led me to a greater understanding about myself, and I knew that over-consuming wine only enabled those old feelings and beliefs. When I reached my truth, I let go of all that no longer served me as if I'd breathed it into a balloon and released it to the universe. Where I was once on a nonstop merry-go-round searching for approval and acceptance, I was now grounded, focused and liberated. My truth became my sense of belonging to myself.

Self-Care and Positive Affirmations

Affirmations are those things you tell yourself about yourself and what you're doing. They can be negative, such as "I am tired, grumpy, upset." Chances are, if you are telling yourself these things, then you are. Or they can be positive, such as "I feel happy, energized, inspired, grateful!" These are positive affirmations of the best kind.

Try telling yourself right now how happy, energized, inspired and grateful you are. Say it out loud and don't forget to smile. Every morning after you get up and every evening just before bed, look into a mirror and tell yourself positive affirmations. You'll be amazed how good you feel.

You may feel uncomfortable at first. That's just your ego trying to control you. Ignore it. Ego is like the hairy little beast on my kitchen island. Whenever I feel ego taking hold of me, I visualize myself as Jeannie from that great old TV show *I Dream of Jeannie*. All I need to do is nod and blink, and ego disappears.

Even if you don't feel positive vibes when you first practise positive affirmations, through daily practice you may find yourself giggling at your own grumpy reflection. Release your ego. Go ahead, throw your head back and laugh out loud. You will feel completely free.

Dear Reader

It is my sincere hope that this book has transformed your life by helping you realize that you are not powerless—over wine, food or any other habit you may have. You *can* take back control and enjoy wine in moderation. The choice is yours. It all begins with self-care, a whole lot of love and believing in your inner wisdom and personal power. You deserve to be happy, healthy and loved. I thank you for taking your first step by reading this book, and I wish you well along the path to your comfort zone.

Writing this book has been an incredible reawakening of my inner spirit. Through the power of self-love, I have overcome my fears about sharing my personal relationship with wine. Many times I felt as if I was jumping out of a plane, uncertain where I'd land. It wasn't long before I realized it didn't matter. All my life, I've landed on my feet, and always where I was meant to. I trusted my intuition and my inner voice and allowed myself to be guided. I hope you can too.

I have no regrets about exposing my little secret to the world—that I've been a closet wine drinker for at least a decade. Now I enjoy my intimate, uncomplicated relationship with wine. I trust that this book has led you to reclaim your power to enjoy everything positive that wine has to offer, in moderation and within your comfort zone.

My Comfort Zone

I carry the following acronym with me at all times. It is a pleasant reminder of where I am, right now, within my comfort zone.

C   Centered awareness: I am harmoniously centered and aware.
O   Optimism: I live each day with optimism.
M   Mindful: I am mindful of body, mind and spirit.
F   Free: I am free to choose.
O   Own: I own the consequences of my actions.
R   Reconnect: I reconnect with my inner wisdom, my truth.
T   Transformation: I welcome positive transformation.
Z   Zone: I live within my own comfort zone.
O   Option: I always have an option.
N   Nourish: I nourish my mind, body and spirit with truth.
E   Embrace: I embrace my inner wisdom.

I didn't reach my comfort zone until I had practised each of the points in this book many, many times. Take each one, on its own, and over the next couple of weeks spend one day practising what it means in your life. After a few weeks of this, you will begin to notice a new level of conscious awareness that will keep you within your comfort zone.

Comfort Journal Prompt

Warm-Up Activity

Think about how you will stay on track and what you can do as a reminder of how far you've come. Remember the message in the bottle you wrote in chapter six? Imagine yourself on that same beach walking along the shoreline. You spot the same bottle. A small wave carries it toward you, delivering it gently to your feet. You pick it up in anxious anticipation to reread your message. You twist the cork and open it. You turn the bottle upside down and shake it, ready to catch the message. The bottle is empty.

Comfort Journal Entry

The message you wrote has been delivered. How do you feel? Write a message of gratitude to your inner guide. Place this new message in the bottle, seal it and toss it as far as you can, into the ocean.

———•◦•———

Notes

Web addresses cited in these notes were current at the time this book was published but may have changed.

Chapter 1, Comfort Zone

O, The Oprah Magazine, August 2013, http://www.oprah.com/health/ Alcohol-and-Your-Health-Dr-Ozs-Rules-for-Safe-Drinking

Chapter 3, Detox

Applications for devices to monitor and track alcohol consumption can be found at these websites: http://drinkcontrolapp.com/; https://play. google.com/store/apps/details?id=org.M.alcodroid; http://www. slappme.com/

Hollis, Jack F., et al, "Weight Loss During the Intensive Intervention Phase of the Weight-Loss Maintenance Trial," *American Journal of Preventive Medicine*, 35, no. 2 (August 2008), 118–126, http://www.ajpmonline. org/article/S0749-3797%2808%2900374-7/abstract

Chapter 6, Know Your Limit, Wine Within It

Canada's Low-Risk Alcohol Drinking Guidelines, http://www.ccsa.ca/ Resource%20Library/2012-Canada-Low-Risk-Alcohol-Drinking-Guidelines-Brochure-en.pdf

Glaser, Gabrielle, *Her Best-Kept Secret: Why Women Drink—And How They Can Regain Control*, New York: Simon & Shuster, 2013.

Miller, William R. and Ricardo F. Muñoz, *Controlling Your Drinking: Tools to Make Moderation Work for You*, New York: Guilford Press, 2013.

Peele, Stanton and Ilse Thompson, *Recover! Stop Thinking Like an Addict and Reclaim Your Life with The Perfect Program*, Boston: Da Capo Press, 2014.

Chapter 7, Social Lubrication

Urban Dictionary, definition of social lubrication: http://www. urbandictionary.com/define.php?term=social%20lubricant

Chapter 8, Fishbowl Margaritas

Canada's Low-Risk Alcohol Drinking Guidelines, http://www.ccsa.ca/Resource%20Library/2012-Canada-Low-Risk-Alcohol-Drinking-Guidelines-Brochure-en.pdf

Walker, D., et al, "Half Full or Empty: Cues That Lead Wine Drinkers to Unintentionally Overpour," *Substance Use & Misuse*, 49, no. 3 (2013), 295–302, http://foodpsychology.cornell.edu/op/wine

Chapter 12, Self-Care

Bell, Katie Kelly, "Are You Drinking Too Much? The Myth of Moderation," Forbes, September 3, 2013, http://www.forbes.com/sites/katiebell/2013/09/03/are-you-drinking-too-much-the-myth-of-moderation/

Dawes, Susan, *When Mom's Happy Everyone's Happy: A Guide for Improving Self-Identity and Relationships*, New York: Cardinal House Publishing, 1998.

Additional Resources

BAC Estimation Table: http://casaa.unm.edu/BACTable/

Definition of moderation, Free Dictionary: http://www.thefreedictionary.com/moderation

Fancy Pants Wine: http://www.fancypantswines.com/?ag=1

"Know Your Limit, Drink Within It," adapted from B.C. Lottery Corporation, "Know your limit, play within it."

Skinnygirl Cocktails and Wine: http://skinnygirlcocktails.com/lpa

"Why Limit Happy to an Hour?" Found on coasters at Pier One, Pitt Meadows, B.C. Canada

Wine quotes: https://www.goodreads.com/quotes/tag/wine

About the Author

Marla O'Brien is a writer, blogger and retired teacher. She holds a post-graduate diploma in educational technology, a diploma in health and fitness studies, and professional teaching certification. A teacher and teacher-librarian for 25 years and a community services coordinator, Marla O'Brien has served as a mentor in education, health and fitness, spiritual  well-being, and reclaiming inner power over wine. She lives in Maple Ridge, British Columbia, with her husband, Tim, and little dog Minnie.